CAMPAIGN 307

FONTENOY 1745

Cumberland's Bloody Defeat

MICHAEL MCNALLY   ILLUSTRATED BY SEÁN Ó'BRÓGÁIN

Series editor Marcus Cowper

First published in Great Britain in 2017 by Osprey Publishing,
PO Box 883, Oxford, OX1 9PL, UK
1385 Broadway, 5th Floor, New York, NY 10018, USA
E-mail: info@ospreypublishing.com

Osprey Publishing, part of Bloomsbury Publishing Plc

A CIP catalogue record for this book is available from the British Library.

Print ISBN: 9781472816252
PDF e-book ISBN: 9781472816276
ePub e-book ISBN: 9781472816269
XML ISBN: 9781472822673

Index by Zoe Hall
Typeset in Myriad Pro and Sabon
Maps by Bounford.com
3D BEVs by The Black Spot
Originated by PDQ Media, Bungay, UK
Printed in China through World Print Ltd.

17 18 19 20 21 10 9 8 7 6 5 4 3 2 1

DEDICATION

This book is dedicated to the memory of F. Glenn Thompson – artist,
scholar, historian – who was sadly taken from us as the book was
nearing completion.

AUTHOR'S NOTE

As always, I would like to firstly thank my wife – Petra – and children –
Stephen, Elena and Liam – for their continued support whilst indulging my
hobby. Next I would like to express my gratitude to Seán Ó'Brógáin, Andy
Copestake, Iain Stanford and Robert Hall, fellow historians and partners in
crime for being there when I needed to talk theories through.
The beauty of writing for Osprey is that it gives me the opportunity to meet
and correspond with people with similar interests and I'd like to express my
gratitude to the following: in Belgium, Alain Bonnet and Alain Tripnaux for
their fantastic welcome at Fontenoy and also for taking the time to show
both Séan and myself around the battlefield; to Charles Deligne of the
Musée d'Armes et d'Histoire militaire in Tournai, firstly for a personal guided
tour of the museum and the extant defences of the town, and secondly for
granting permission for the reproduction of a number of images from
Tournai, Fontenoy 1745 – Un siège, une bataille; in Dublin, Lar Joye of the
National Museum of Ireland, for his advice and kind permission to
reproduce an image of the sole surviving battalion colour, carried by the
Dillon regiment at Fontenoy; in France, David Wilson for a regular
correspondence and for kind permission to use the manuscript of the
second edition of his *The French Army of the War of the Austrian Succession –
1740–1748* as part of my research; in Italy, Gabriele Mendella for his kind
permission to reproduce a number of images from his exhibition and
accompanying book *La Maison du Roy*; in the Netherlands, Jurrien de Jong
for helping with various queries on the Dutch forces; finally, in Austria, my
heartfelt thanks to Douglas O'Donell for his help in sourcing a copy of the
elusive ninth volume of the *Österreichischer Erbfolge Krieg 1740–48*.

ARTIST'S NOTE

Readers may care to note that the original paintings from which the colour
plates in this book were prepared are available for private sale. The
Publishers retain all reproduction copyright whatsoever. All enquiries
should be addressed to:

seanobrogain@yahoo.ie

The Publishers regret that they can enter into no correspondence upon
this matter.

EDITOR'S NOTE

Unless otherwise indicated, all the images in this book are part of the
author's collection.

Osprey Publishing supports the Woodland Trust, the UK's leading woodland
conservation charity. Between 2014 and 2018 our donations are being
spent on their Centenary Woods project in the UK.

To find out more about our authors and books visit
www.ospreypublishing.com. Here you will find extracts, author
interviews, details of forthcoming events and the option to sign up for
our newsletter.

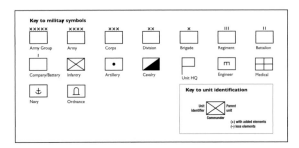

CONTENTS

Western Europe showing political affiliations in 1740

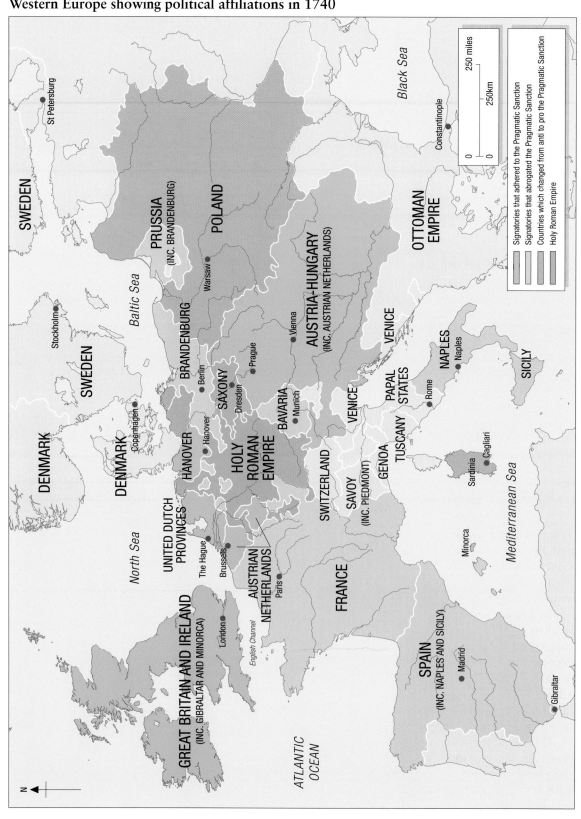

THE STRATEGIC SITUATION

On 20 October 1740 Charles VI, the Holy Roman Emperor, died in Vienna, and his passing would cause another of the 18th century's succession crises. As a teenager he had been the original Habsburg candidate during the War of the Spanish Succession, but in 1711 he succeeded to the Imperial Throne, as the sole male Habsburg heir, superseding the claims of his two nieces Maria-Josepha and Maria-Amalia.

In 1713, and concerned by his wife's inability to produce a male heir, he arranged for promulgation of an agreement known as the Pragmatic Sanction, which allowed for the future succession through the female line if there were no eligible male heir. The agreement made provision solely for his line and not that of his elder brother, effectively negating an agreement that he had signed upon his accession by excluding his nieces from the succession and sowing the seeds of the future conflict.

After several years' hard negotiation Charles achieved his aims; the principal European states signed their agreement to the pact, and in 1717 the Habsburg succession descended upon the newly born Archduchess Maria Theresia. After the princess's birth, several more years of intense discussions took place as the crowned heads of Europe sought further inducements to ensure that they stuck to their agreements.

With the Emperor's death this diplomatic house of cards collapsed with Saxony-Poland (whose King, Augustus III, was married to Maria-Josepha) and Bavaria (whose Duke, the Elector Charles Albert was married to Maria-Amalia) both reneging on the agreement in order to pursue their wives' claims, whilst France and Spain – ever keen to weaken the Habsburgs – declared their support for Bavaria. On the sidelines, the ever-opportunistic Frederick II of Prussia, declared for his own interests by taking advantage of the political vacuum and invading the Austrian province of Silesia on 8 November.

The initial stages of the War of the Austrian Succession (1741–48) saw the Habsburgs firmly on the back foot with Prussia consolidating her hold on Silesia, and the Franco-Bavarians and

Memorial plaque raised to commemorate the regiments of the British Army that fought at Fontenoy. At the time of the battle the regiments were known by name, normally that of their colonel, and the later numerical designations – where applicable – are noted next to each unit's title.

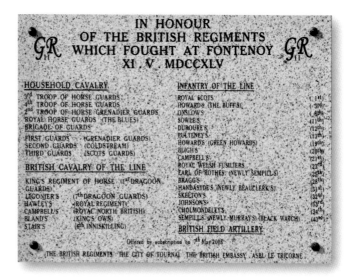

IN HONOUR
OF THE BRITISH REGIMENTS
G R WHICH FOUGHT AT FONTENOY G R
XI . V . MDCCXLV

HOUSEHOLD CAVALRY

INFANTRY OF THE LINE

BRITISH CAVALRY OF THE LINE

BRITISH FIELD ARTILLERY

Saxons both seeking to annex Bohemia. It was a confusing campaign based upon political rather than military objectives whereby a Franco-Bavarian army halted its advance on the Austrian capital and, ignoring a virtually undefended Vienna, raced instead to thwart a Saxon attack on Prague. Thanks to the intervention of Maurice de Saxe, three of whose half-brothers commanded the Saxon Army, the city was taken by escalade with minimal casualties, but it was a fleeting success and much of the province was recaptured by the Austrians during the spring and summer of 1742.

The following year, the focal point of the conflict was the battle of Dettingen where a French Army under Noailles had attempted to trap a British-led Allied army under King George II of England, the manoeuvre failing when the Duc de Grammont – in command of a blocking force – chose to abandon his position and attack the enemy, instead of remaining on the defensive and waiting for Noailles to arrive and take them in the rear. The conduct of the battle would remain a 'running sore' for many of the combatants, and it would still resonate at Fontenoy two years later.

By 1744, the main theatre of operations had switched to Austria and Central Germany, and the French were forced to detach over half of the Army of Flanders to Alsace in order to contain a major enemy incursion and it was left to the newly promoted Marshal Maurice de Saxe to defend Flanders with 50,000 men against an Allied army that outnumbered him over two to one.

The Allied commander – Field Marshal George Wade – was, like many of his peers, a soldier who had learned his trade under Eugene and Marlborough, and thus his plan of campaign was a relatively simple one, based upon his taking the field with a massive numerical superiority and then laying siege to and capturing the important French fortress of Lille, a feat which would not only compromise the enemy position in Flanders, but would also provide a springboard for a later advance on Paris.

The Allied campaign had started promisingly enough, but Saxe refused to remain passive in defence and harried the enemy constantly, keeping them off balance. And as the Allies stalled before Lille without actually starting formal siege operations, confidence in Wade's ability began to ebb steadily. On one occasion, when a French raiding party overran the Allied headquarters, one officer commented that the biggest mistake Saxe could make would be actually to capture Wade. Having seemingly surrendered the initiative, the Allies remained stalled before their objective for several weeks and sickness and disease soon began to rage throughout the army, obliging Wade to concede defeat and withdraw early into winter quarters, leaving Saxe and his reputation in the ascendant.

Leaving the army covering the approaches to Brussels before going into winter quarters, Wade retired to Antwerp where he wrote to King George II asking that he be relieved of his command. The request was grudgingly accepted and a search undertaken for a suitable successor. The initial choice was for a reinstatement of Wade's predecessor, the Earl of Stair, but he was unwilling to accept and so the net was cast wider, the main prerogative being that the candidate had to outrank his allied compatriots in order to retain the senior command and ensure that British interests were maintained. In the end, there was but one choice – albeit a popular one – the king's second

The image of a Warrior King. This martial image of King Louis XV by Maurice Quentin de la Tour is how the French monarch would have liked himself to be viewed by his subjects. Many contemporary sketches tend to show him in a less flattering light.

son, William Augustus, Duke of Cumberland. As colonel of the First Foot Guards and ranking as a lieutenant-general on the regular establishment, he had served with distinction at Dettingen and, moreover, was well thought of by his peers. Consultations with Britain's allies quickly took place, and Cumberland was confirmed as 'Captain-General of His Majesty's Forces serving in Europe' and thus commander of the Pragmatic Army, being given leave to organize his affairs before taking up his appointment prior to the beginning of the 1745 campaigning season.

From his headquarters at Lille, and convinced that the key to a French victory lay more than ever with a conquest of Flanders, Saxe now began planning for a military operation which would 'draw the teeth' of the enemy hydra. With more senior French generals having been less than successful in Germany, Louis XV was now more than willing to listen to Saxe's plans for the concentration of France's best troops to take part in an offensive which, beginning earlier than the normally accepted start to the campaigning season, would catch the enemy off guard whilst they were still dispersed for the winter and achieve its objectives before they could set their own plans in motion, thereby gaining and retaining the strategic initiative.

CHRONOLOGY

1700–15	War of the Spanish Succession.
1711	Charles von Habsburg crowned Holy Roman Emperor as Charles VI.
1713	Charles VI disinherits his nieces and promulgates the 'Pragmatic Sanction' in order to secure a possible female succession through his own line.
1716	Birth, and death, of the Archduke Leopold Johann.
1717	Birth of the Archduchess Maria Theresia, future Empress.
1740	Death of Charles VI.
	Bavaria, France, Prussia, Saxony and Spain abrogate the 'Pragmatic Sanction'. Prussia invades Silesia.
1741	Beginning of the War of the Austrian Succession.
1742	Capture of Prague.
	Charles Albert of Bavaria crowned Holy Roman Emperor as Charles VII.
1743	Battle of Dettingen.
1744	Wade's failed campaign in Flanders.
	Saxe submits his plan for the French conquest of the Austrian Netherlands.

1745

13 April	Saxe issues instructions for the concentration of the Army of Flanders.
26 April	French forces under Brézé begin siege of Tournai.
28 April	Saxe arrives at Tournai with bulk of the Army of Flanders.
29–30 April	Pragmatic Army leaves Anderlecht in pursuit of Saxe.
5 May	Skirmish at Leuze.
7 May	Pragmatic Army arrives at Moulbaix.
8 May	Pragmatic Army arrives at Maubray.
	Saxe makes initial deployments around Fontenoy sector.
9 May	French conduct detailed reconnaissance of Fontenoy area.
	Pragmatic Army remains encamped in the Maubray–Wasmes area.
10 May	Army of Flanders takes up battle positions around Fontenoy sector.
	Work commences on series of redoubts to strengthen French positions.
	Both sides conduct a series of reconnaissances of enemy positions and hold final councils of war – Cumberland commits himself to attack the enemy the following morning.
11 May	The battle of Fontenoy.
	The defeated Allies retreat to Ath.

OPPOSING COMMANDERS

THE FRENCH

Armand Maurice, Comte de Saxe, Marshal of France (1696–1750)
The eldest of Augustus II of Saxony's extensive brood of illegitimate children, Maurice was the closest in temperament to his father and it was no surprise that he was permitted to join the military whilst in his early teens, seeing extensive service in the Imperialist forces of Eugene of Savoy, his experiences ranging from Malplaquet in 1709 to the siege of Belgrade in 1717.

Returning from the wars to the threat of an arranged marriage, Saxe fled at the first opportunity setting out for Paris, where he soon used his contacts from Imperial service to secure a commission in the French Army, ultimately purchasing the colonelcy of the Régiment de Greder, a crack unit once commanded by his maternal grandfather, Karl von Königsmarck.

Eventually becoming bored with Paris, he sold the regiment to one of his many half-brothers, using the sale to fund a journey to Courland, an electoral duchy on the Baltic, where he hoped to be elected Duke as the male line of the ruling family of the duchy was threatened with extinction, and it was here that he received two further offers of marriage – one from the Princess Elizabeth Petrovna, daughter of Peter the Great, and one from the Duchess Anna Ivanova, de facto Duchess of Courland. Choosing the Duchess over the Princess, Saxe was successful in his election but the political intrigues of the Saxo-Polish court, and violent disagreements with the Duchess Anna led to a Russian intervention in Courland, whereby it was suggested that he vacate the region or 'be transported to a landscape with a wider horizon' i.e. Siberia. The irony in the affair being that Anna ascended to the Russian throne in 1730, being succeeded by Elizabeth in 1741.

Eventually returning to Paris, he found that his Baltic exploits had only added lustre to his reputation and, as a result, he was a prominent fixture in the negotiations with Berlin aimed at forestalling an Austro-Russian entente, the objective of which was the dismemberment of Poland. Attempts by Augustus to wean his son away from French service foundered for, as he was to write himself, 'Who would wish to serve as a Field Marshal in the Saxon army, when he could be a captain in the army of France?'

Augustus's death in 1733 led to the second of the 18th-century 'Wars of Succession', and again Maurice rebuffed overtures which would see him appointed commander-in-chief of the Saxon Army, preferring to remain a colonel in the French service, certain that his currency would rise faster in

Maurice de Saxe by Johan Georg Wille (after Rigaud). By far France's best battlefield commander of the period, Saxe was given the senior command in 1745 as a testament to both his ability and his relationship with King Louis XV. At Fontenoy, he was required to fight not only against the Allies, but also against severe ill health and his inveterate rivals at the French court in order to gain victory. His management of the ever-shifting battlefield situation led to Napoleon Bonaparte later calling him one of the greatest captains of history.

this way than in any other. In this he was to be proved prescient, serving with distinction under the Marshals Berwick, Asfeld and Noailles in succession, receiving his coveted promotion to lieutenant-general on 1 August 1734. The following month the French Army went into winter quarters, and on 5 November an armistice was signed – the War of the Polish Succession was over.

For the next few years Maurice drifted, alternating between Parisian society and his brother's court in Dresden, even making a second – and again abortive – attempt to secure the throne of Courland, but the death of the Emperor Charles VI, in October 1740, meant but one thing: a return to active service.

In the first years of the new conflict, Maurice continued to show his quality in comparison with his peers, irrespective of which side they fought on – he masterminded the capture of Prague in 1741, and in the wake of a resurgent Austrian *reconquista* in Bohemia and Bavaria he ensured that the French border remained inviolate, performing prodigious feats whilst often outnumbered and outgunned by the enemy. But it was in 1744 when his star finally rose, firstly on 26 March, when he was created a Marshal of France, and then with less than 50,000 men he thwarted the attempts of the Allies to capture Lille and overrun northern France. By this success, together with a series of personal alliances that he had been forging since the outbreak of hostilities, he secured the senior command in what was to become the crucial theatre of operations for 1745, a campaign that would serve finally to cement his position within the French military.

Ulrich Friedrich Waldemar, Comte de Löwendahl (1700–55)

In many ways, Löwendahl's career would mirror that of his friend and mentor, Maurice de Saxe, with his entering the Imperial service at the youthful age of 13 and being promoted to captain the following year when he transferred to the Danish Army. It was to prove the beginning of a journey which would see him serve several military masters.

Rejoining the Imperial Army in 1716, Löwendahl distinguished himself at the battles of Peterwardein and Temesvár (both 1716) and the capture of Belgrade in the following year. With the capture of the city, and by now serving as a captain of grenadiers, he moved to the Italian theatre before eventually transferring to the Saxon service in 1722 as a colonel, and over the next few years his regiment became a byword for meticulous drill, much like the Régiment de Saxe in French service.

Perhaps influenced by Maurice de Saxe in his visits to Dresden, the Saxon Crown soon began to take notice of the half-Danish officer and by the early 1730s he had been promoted to Field Marshal and Inspector General of the

Saxon Infantry. During the early part of the War of the Polish Succession, Löwendahl oversaw the defence of Krakow against the insurgent forces, and in 1734 was sent to command the Saxon forces in the Rhineland.

After the end of hostilities, Löwendahl moved into the Russian service, fighting against the Turks at Khotyn in 1739, and then against the Swedes in the Baltic from 1741 to 1743 where he gained the favour of the Empress Elizabeth, at which time he entered into correspondence with Saxe to sound him out about the possibility of his being able to secure a commission in French service.

The positive answer was tempered by the fact that Löwendahl would have to take a demotion and become the most junior lieutenant-general on the service list and in September 1743 he made the transfer that would – like Saxe – define his military career, being simultaneously authorized to raise a 'German' regiment which would bear his name.

Löwendahl's service for his adopted country was as conscientious as his sponsor's and he was soon known to the French court as the captor of Menin, Ypres and Freiburg, and so, when Saxe asked specifically for his attachment to the Army of Flanders for his proposed campaign in 1745, the request was readily granted by King Louis XV and at Fontenoy, Sluys, Ghent, Oudenaarde and several other engagements he was to prove his worth as both an able subordinate and a trusted independent commander. Indeed it was in this role that he was to receive his highest praise and greatest damnation when, in September 1747, he stormed the seemingly impregnable Dutch fortress of Bergen-op-Zoom and gave the town over to two days of pillage.

Although there is little corroborative evidence, tradition has it that Saxe placed the blame for the debacle firmly on his friend's shoulders, writing to the king at Versailles, 'Majesty, for the events at Bergen, you have but one of two choices – either to hang him as an example or to make him a Marshal of France'. Löwendahl received his Marshal's baton the same year.

THE ALLIES

Prince William Augustus KG, KB, FRS, Duke of Cumberland (1721–65)
The sixth child, and second surviving son of King George II of England, Cumberland was the eldest of those of the royal children born in London rather than Hanover and, as such, came to be regarded by his father as the key to the complicated political intrigues which had for more than a decade soured the relationship between the King and his eldest son Friedrich-Ludwig, the future Prince of Wales.

Rapidly becoming his parents' favourite, William was enrolled in the 2nd Foot Guards (Coldstreams) and was created a Knight of the Bath at the tender age of four; one year later he was invested with several titles, the principal of which being Duke of Cumberland, the title by which he is generally known.

Growing up, and despite his family's Germanic ties, Cumberland viewed himself as being first and foremost an Englishman and this would explain his father's plans for him firstly to become Lord High Admiral of England, and secondly – if a constitutional method could be found – for him to become Prince of Wales in place of his brother, who would receive the Electorate of Hanover. Ultimately both plans came to nothing, the first when the 19-year-old

William Augustus, Duke of Cumberland – after Sir Joshua Reynolds. King George II's favourite son – his 'martial boy' – Cumberland was unfortunate to meet France's best general at the height of his powers. Criticized for his inexperience at senior command, and later damned for his conduct at Culloden in 1746, many eyewitnesses of the battle of Fontenoy cite his bravery and coolness under fire as being one of the deciding factors which prevented the disintegration of the Anglo-Hanoverian withdrawal into a disastrous rout.

prince, after serving as a volunteer in the Channel Fleet elected for a career in the Army, and the second through the unwillingness of his elder brother to accept what was, in effect, a demotion in the line of succession.

In February 1741, Cumberland was appointed Colonel of the 1st Foot Guards (Grenadiers), transferring from his previous regiment and, by the close of the following year, he was promoted to major-general. It was clear to all observers that the 'phoney war' that had been in place since the outbreak of the War of the Austrian Succession (Britain/Hanover and France served solely as auxiliaries of Austria and Bavaria respectively, rather than as belligerents) would soon be over, and both King George and the Duke now joined the Allied Army in the field.

The campaign almost turned into disaster at Dettingen when the army was trapped against the Main by a superior French Army, but the Allied Army fought their way through the French blocking force and made its way to safety. Wounded in the leg, Cumberland impressed observers with his conduct and calmness under fire, and in the aftermath of battle he was promoted to lieutenant-general.

In 1744, Cumberland was given command of the forces to defend the country against an anticipated Jacobite invasion, and when this threat never materialized the Duke began to petition his father for a senior position within the British Army in Flanders. After much negotiation, and in the face of much opposition, he was appointed 'Captain-General of His Majesty's land forces which are or shall be employed abroad in conjunction with the forces of His Majesty's allies', effectively commander of all Allied forces within the theatre of operations.

Although relatively inexperienced, the new commander could rely on the advice of a number of veteran officers such as Sir John Ligonier or Sir James Campbell, in addition to which he had assembled an excellent staff and any perceived insufficiencies would certainly be resolved before any lasting damage could be done. All in all, he was as prepared as he could be for the coming campaign, with the cachet of his rank serving to ease most, but unfortunately not all, of the tensions between the Allied partners.

Karl August Friedrich, Fürst von Waldeck-Pyrmont (1704–63)

The second son of Friedrich-Anton-Ulrich, Graf von Waldeck-Pyrmont, Waldeck was born into a German family with a long tradition of foreign military service; initially he saw active duty in the French Army, before accepting a commission as a junior officer in the Prussian service.

In 1728 this duty was suspended on the deaths of his father and elder brother and he acceded to the family dignity of Count and Prince of Waldeck-Pyrmont. During the War of the Polish Succession (1733–38) he fought with the Imperial Army with the rank of *Generalfeldwachtmeister* – roughly equivalent to major-general – and served on the Rhine under Prince Eugene of Savoy, distinguishing himself at the battle of Klausen on 20 October 1735. The following year, Waldeck transferred to the Balkan front, serving with distinction against the Turks, and was promoted to lieutenant-general on 21 March 1738. The following year he took part in and was wounded at the disastrous battle of Grocka, which led to the surrender of Belgrade and a reversal of all the territorial gains that Austria had made under Eugene. His role in the defeat was to have no adverse effect on his career, however, and in November 1741 he received a promotion to general of infantry (*Feldzeugmeister*).

Three years later, and possibly in acknowledgement of his father's previous service, Waldeck was appointed Commanding General of the Dutch Army at the relatively young age of 38. Although the United Dutch Provinces had a long tradition of employing foreign generals, it was a controversial decision and many believed that other candidates such as the octogenarian Isaac Kock van Cronström, who at least was married to a Dutch woman, would have been more suitable. This controversy would dog Waldeck throughout his tenure of command and is undoubtedly a contributing factor in the problems which split the Allied high command in 1745.

Waldeck's command at Fontenoy has often been described as 'lacklustre', but like Saxe he had to fight both the enemy and his subordinate commanders at the same time, and, unlike his colleagues on the Allied right flank, he was able to disengage cleanly from the battlefield whilst conducting a textbook manoeuvre – withdrawing his artillery and infantry in sequence whilst covering the movement with as much of his cavalry as he could rally – and despite the defeat he was appointed an Imperial Field Marshal in March 1746, remaining in command of the Dutch forces throughout that year.

In 1747, the defeat at Lauffeldt signalled the end of Waldeck's career in Dutch service. Voices that had been raised against him since he had initially accepted the command were now supported by those who were simply unhappy and disillusioned with the physical and financial cost of the war and William IV, the Prince of Orange, felt he had no other option than to release him from duty.

Joseph Lothar Dominik, Graf von Königsegg-Rothenfels (1673–1751)

The seventh son of his father's first marriage, Königsegg was – like many younger children from his background – originally intended for a career in the Church, having been sent to the Jesuit seminary at Besançon in France before taking up service with the Archbishop of Salzburg. An appointment as Papal chamberlain had also been arranged for him, but he felt that he was best suited to serve God in another fashion, and so he left Rome and made his way to Hungary where he enlisted in the Imperial Army, then fighting against the Turks, serving in the cuirassier regiment 'Hohenzollern' for the next eight years.

Königsegg fought under Eugene in Northern Italy during the War of the Spanish Succession (1701–14), was promoted to colonel in October 1702 and received command of his own infantry regiment the following January. Promotion to *Generalfeldwachtmeister* (1705) and lieutenant-general (1708) soon followed, the latter as a result of his distinguished service at the battle of Turin (1706). At the end of the war he demonstrated his flair for diplomacy by taking a leading part in the peace negotiations, being rewarded with the command of the Imperial forces in the newly created Austrian Netherlands.

In 1717, Königsegg was promoted to general of infantry and, after a short interlude in which he undertook several diplomatic missions, he was promoted to field marshal in October 1723 and appointed vice-president of the Imperial War Council in 1728.

The War of the Polish Succession saw him once more in Northern Italy, where he assumed command of the Imperial forces upon the death of the Graf von Mercy and, despite initial successes against the Franco-Hispano-Savoyard forces, a lack of resources meant that the Austrians were ultimately pushed back into the Tyrol and Königsegg obliged to lay down his command, and it looked as if Königsegg's active service was over when he assumed the presidency of the Imperial War Council in 1736.

His decision to come out of semi-retirement in 1737 and assume personal command of the Imperial forces fighting the Turks proved to be an unmitigated disaster – leading ultimately to the debacle at Grocka – and he was forced to step down from all military duties, an act which inadvertently saved him from being tried and imprisoned at the end of hostilities, as were many of his peers and former subordinates.

With the outbreak of the War of the Austrian Succession, Königsegg's role was mainly of a diplomatic nature, and in 1744 he was briefly appointed Military Governor of Vienna before assuming command of the Imperial forces in the Austrian Netherlands, a posting that many believed was nothing more than a provincial backwater, the hitherto principal theatres of operations having been Germany and Bohemia/Silesia.

As an Imperial Field Marshal, Königsegg was Cumberland's senior subordinate and thus ranked as *ad latus* which is often erroneously translated as 'deputy' rather than 'adjutant' which is closer to the dictionary definition. In practice, and given the relatively small number of Austrian troops which took the field with the Pragmatic Army, Königsegg should perhaps be seen as the Captain-General's 'principal adviser'.

OPPOSING FORCES

THE ALLIES

The Pragmatic Army of 1745 was a flawed weapon – its area of operations meant that it consisted of several nationalities, the aims of whose respective governments did not always facilitate a common policy. Ruled from Vienna, it was obvious that Austrian troops would be deployed to defend the Austrian Netherlands, whilst as a result of the Barrier Treaties of 1709–15 the Dutch were granted the right to garrison a series of fortified towns in the region in order to protect against French invasion. The British and Hanoverians were later deployed there as a deterrent against any French moves to isolate the Electorate of Hanover, the ruler of which was simultaneously King of England. As such, it needed to be led by a forceful personality who would brook neither disobedience nor dissent in his subordinates.

At the highest level, Cumberland's inexperience would, on the whole, prove to be a liability, whilst the Dutch commanders were bitterly divided amongst themselves, the sole point of unity being the general opposition over the appointment of Waldeck to the command of the forces of the States General. On a lower level, Waldeck mistrusted not only the commitment of his subordinates but also – with notable exceptions – the commitment and ability of his own troops. Elsewhere the antipathy of the British towards the Hanoverian contingent was palpable, fuelled by their resentment at what they perceived to have been Hanoverian duplicity at Dettingen. The only contingent to escape from the opprobrium were the Austrians, and this had possibly as much to do with their relative lack of numbers as with any respect in which Königsegg was held by his peers.

Organizationally, the army also suffered as a result of Saxe's misinformation – believing that Saxe had committed only 30,000 troops to field operations, Cumberland felt that the forces he was able to assemble at Anderlecht would be more than sufficient to defeat the French, and it was only after the perceived threat to Mons was dispelled that he drew upon allied garrisons (Mons and Ath) to strengthen his own army – of the four strongest garrisons in Flanders, Tournai was under siege whilst Luxembourg was too far away, but between them both Charleroi and Namur could easily have provided several thousand fresh troops without compromising their integrity. It was a reinforcement that would be greatly missed at Fontenoy, not merely in addressing the later perceived disparity in numbers, but also

British infantry swords 1742–51. Effectively a solid brass hilt fixed to the blade, many soldiers viewed them as an encumbrance rather than a useful weapon. (Image copyright and reproduced with kind permission of the Musée d'Histoire militaire de la Ville de Tournai)

in the added tactical flexibility that they would have given Cumberland in his plan of attack.

On the field of Fontenoy, the Pragmatic Army deployed some 46 battalions of foot – in the main, and with the exception of the Swiss in Dutch service, each regiment would have equated to a single battalion with a field strength of *c*.650 men divided into 10–12 companies, depending on nationality, of which one company would be equipped as grenadiers. A notable exception to this was the British Guards whose field strength would have been more in the region of 1,000 effectives. All troops would have been armed with a smoothbore musket with triangular bayonet and possibly a short sword or 'hanger' for the 'hatmen' and a small hatchet for the grenadiers, but again calibre of weapon and the number of prepared cartridges and powder and ball would have varied greatly from nationality to nationality. The British infantry would have formed in longer, shallower formations, allowing a greater number of weapons to be brought to bear when firing upon the enemy, whilst the Dutch and possibly Hanoverians would have deployed deeper, reducing the area that the units occupied and relying on the weight of manpower to decide the issue of combat.

The 91 squadrons of cavalry were divided between the regiments of horse, mounted on heavier horses and generally armed with a straight-bladed

Although not part of the Royal Household, the red-coated Gendarmerie de France were nonetheless the elite of the line cavalry, but organized on a company rather than a regimental basis. This reconstruction is of the uniform of a trumpeter of the Gendarmerie as would have been worn in 1745. (Image copyright and reproduced with kind permission of Gabriele Mendella)

sword and a pair of pistols, and the dragoons – able to fight both on horse and foot – who were equipped with a short musket or carbine and possibly a single pistol. Regiments of horse would generally have had a field strength of *c*.300 men divided into three squadrons, whilst dragoons fielded up to five squadrons for a strength of around 500 effectives.

The artillery was divided between the 'train' which consisted of the 'field' artillery, i.e. cannon, formally organized into batteries, and those 'battalion' pieces which were allocated to infantry brigades for close fire support. At Fontenoy, the British train consisted of ten 6lb cannon, ten 3lb cannon and four howitzers, whilst the Dutch comprised six 6lb pieces and likewise four howitzers. A further 29 3lb guns and six 1½lb guns were allocated to the infantry of the right wing and 24 3lb guns to the infantry of the left.

In addition to the above, the Austrians provided two regiments of dragoons and two of hussars, light cavalry equipped in the 'Hungarian style', and two independent companies of foot.

THE FRENCH

On receiving Saxe's proposed plan of operations, King Louis XV's only question was 'How many troops?' The answer was optimistic enough – 120 first-line and 50 second-line battalions with adequate cavalry and artillery support, sufficient to achieve all the planned objectives. Yet these wishes were almost granted in their entirety – 140 battalions with the requisite cavalry and artillery, which not only included some of the premier-line units in the French Army, but also the Brigade des Gardes and the Maison du Roi, the Royal Household troops.

Even taking into account the forces allocated to the siege of Tournai, the French Army that took the field at Fontenoy was still a formidable force, but like the Pragmatic Army it had a weakness. The simple reason for this was that even though Saxe had deployed across the most likely route that the Allies would take, he still had to cover other roads and these positions would need to be manned until the enemy's actual line of attack had been ascertained. As a result, the forces immediately available numbered some 52 battalions of foot, 91 squadrons of horse and 15 of dragoons, together with some 50 light cannon *à la Suédoise* and a similar number of field pieces from the artillery park.

Similar to their enemy counterparts, infantry battalions had a campaign strength in the region of 600 men, although regiments would field anything between one and four battalions, with four units generally being brigaded together – thus the Brigade d'Auvergne consisted of the three battalions of that regiment and the single battalion Régiment Nivernois whilst the Brigade du Roi consisted of all four battalions of that regiment. Unlike the enemy, French battalions consisted of 15 companies, of which one would be designated as grenadiers. Again, and like their contemporaries, the principal armament of the infantry was a smoothbore musket with a triangular bayonet. The calibre of the musket, however, was smaller than that of the British weapon, which meant that, in the chaos of the central combat, Cumberland's troops were able to scavenge the French casualties for ammunition. Depending on the number of men present in the unit, battalions would typically form up between four and six ranks deep.

Aside from the line regiments, the French cavalry at Fontenoy contained almost all of the elite regiments of the mounted arm – the Maison du Roi, the Gendarmerie, the Carabiniers, the Cuirassiers – the former being drawn from the aristocracy, and this would at times exacerbate problems of command and control. At Fontenoy, most regiments comprised four squadrons, at a campaign strength of roughly 400 effectives, the exceptions to this being the Maison and Gendarmerie, the strength of which was accounted in terms of 'companies' each of which, at a higher base establishment than the line, would bring them close to squadron strength, and the Carabiniers who mustered ten

French 1734 pattern cavalry sword. (Image reproduced with kind permission of the Musée d'Histoire militaire de la Ville de Tournai)

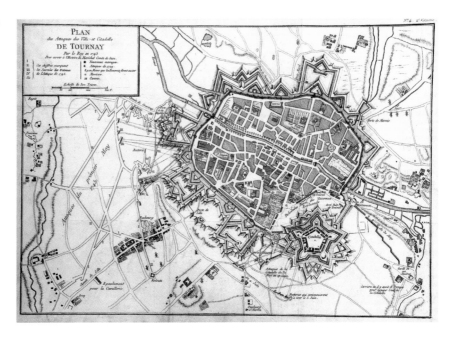

Contemporary plan of the siege of Tournai. The capture of one of the Allies' barrier fortresses was the cornerstone of Saxe's plan of campaign, the bait with which he intended to draw the enemy out of their encampments and force them to give battle relatively early in the campaigning season before they could be reinforced from either Germany or the United Dutch Provinces. He was aided in his task by being able to occupy much of the Marlburian works from the siege of 1709. (Image copyright and reproduced with kind permission of the Musée d'Histoire militaire de la Ville de Tournai)

squadrons. Armament was a straight-bladed heavy cavalry sword with two pistols and a carbine, whilst the Carabiniers and the Mousquetaires du Roi differed by carrying a rifled carbine or short dragoon musket, respectively, together with a bayonet.

Unlike their Allied counterparts who were – to varying degrees – converting to becoming actual cavalry, the French dragoons were just as often called upon to fight dismounted, and it is in this role that Saxe called upon the bulk of his dragoons to serve at Fontenoy, forming a support line for the infantry brigades holding the ridgeline above the Chemin de Condé. Dragoons carried a short dragoon musket with bayonet, a curved light cavalry sword and a pistol.

The one unusual unit attached to Saxe's army were the Arquebusiers de Grassin, raised in 1744 by the Sieur de Grassin, a captain in the Régiment de Picardie. The regiment consisted of nine companies of fusiliers, two of grenadiers and six troops of dragoons. Often referred to as 'light troops', opinion is divided about whether they were deployed primarily as light infantry, similar to the Austrian Jägers, or whether this definition refers to the fact that, unlike the regiments of foot, they had no provision for baggage and therefore travelled 'light'.

French memorial to the dead of Fontenoy. The caption paraphrases King Louis XV's admonishment to the Dauphin on the evening of the battle, and reads: 'The price of victory is measured in blood, and that of our enemies is still the blood of men. The true glory is to spare it.'

II MAI 1745

VOYEZ TOUT LE SANG QUE COUTE UN TRIOMPHE!
LE SANG DE NOS ENNEMIS
EST TOUJOURS LE SANG
DES HOMMES
LA VRAIE GLOIRE C'EST DE L'EPARGNER

Of the 100 guns attached to the army, fully half were deployed as batteries in known positions, whilst the remainder were *pièces á la Suédoise* intended for attachment to infantry formations. Of the former, we know that a significant number of cannon were also deployed to cover the bridgehead at Calonne, in addition to which contemporary plans of the defences of Fontenoy would suggest that during the battle 14 guns were moved into the village during the course of the battle, the last of these being emplaced at around 11.00am, in other words in anticipation of a third attack on the village.

ORDERS OF BATTLE

THE FRENCH ARMY – ARMAND MAURICE, COMTE DE SAXE & MARSHAL OF FRANCE

Brigade de Grassin – Sieur de Grassin
Arquebusiers à pied
Arquebusiers à cheval
Brigade d'Auvergne – Comte de Chabannes
Auvergne (3 battalions)
Nivernois
Brigade de Touraine – Duc de Duras
Touraine (3 battalions)
Brigade d'Eu – Prince de Soubise
Eu (2 battalions)
Angoumois
Royal Corse
Brigade de Normandie – Comte de Talleyrand (KIA at Tournai)
Normandie (4 battalions)
Brigade de Royal Vaisseaux – Comte de Guerchy
Royal Vaisseaux (3 battalions)
Traisnel
Brigade des Irlandais – Comte de Thomond
Bulkeley
Clare
Dillon
Rooth
Berwick
Lally
Brigade de Gardes – Duc de Grammont
Gardes Françaises (4 battalions)
Gardes Suisses (2 battalions)
Brigade d'Aubeterre – Marquis d'Anlézy
Aubeterre
Courten (3 battalions)
Brigade du Roi – Comte de la Serre
Roi (4 battalions)
Brigade du Dauphin – Comte de la Vauguyon
Dauphin (3 battalions)
Beauvoisis
Brigade de Bettens – Marquis de Croissy
Bettens (2 battalions)
Diesbach (3 battalions)
Brigade de Dragons – Marquis de Beauffremont
Maître de Camp (5 squadrons)
Royal (5 squadrons)
Brigade de Dragons – Duc de Chevreuse
Beauffremont (5 squadrons)
Egmont (5 squadrons) – Detached with Comte de Löwendahl
Brigade de Crillon – Comte de la Motte-Hugues
Crillon (3 battalions)
Biron
Brigade de Piémont – Comte de Lorges
Piémont (3 battalions)
Royal le Marine
Brigade de la Couronne – Duc d'Havré
La Couronne (3 battalions)
Soissonais
Brigade Royal – Comte d'Armentières
Royal (3 battalions)
Hainault
Brigade des Royal Cravattes – Comte d'Éstrées
Royal Cravattes (4 squadrons)
Fiennes (4 squadrons)
Brigade de Talleyrand – Comte de Langeron
Orléans (4 squadrons)
Talleyrand (2 squadrons)

Brigade des Cuirassiers – Comte de Löwendahl
Cuirassiers du Roi (4 squadrons)
Egmont (4 squadrons)
Brigade du Colonel-Général – Duc d'Harcourt
Colonel-Général (4 squadrons)
Brancas (4 squadrons)
Brigade de Clermont-Prince – Duc de Penthièvre
Clermont-Prince (4 squadrons)
Fitzjames (4 squadrons)
Brigade du Royal Rousillon – Prince de Pons
Royal Rousillon (4 squadrons)
Prince Camille (4 squadrons)
Brigade de Royal-Étranger – Marquis de Rubenpré
Chabrillant (2 squadrons)
Royal-Étranger (2 squadrons)
Brigade de Brionne – Marquis de Rosen
Brionne (4 squadrons)
Pons (4 squadrons)
Brigade de Noailles – Duc de Boufflers
Noailles (4 squadrons)
Penthiévre (4 squadrons)
Brigade de St Jal – Chevalier d'Aguesseau
Berry (4 squadrons)
Brigade du Roi – Comte de Clérmont-Gallerande
Clermont-Tonnerre (4 squadrons)
du Roi (4 squadrons)
Brigade de Carabiniers – Marquis de Créqui
Royal de Carabiniers (10 squadrons)
Maison du Roi – Comte de Montmorency-Logny
Gardes du Corps (4 Companies)
Gendarmes de la Garde
Chevaulégers de la Garde
Mousquetaires de la Garde (2 companies)
Grenadiers à Cheval
Gendarmerie de France
Gendarmes Ecossais/Gendarmes de Bretagne
Gendarmes Anglais/Chevaulégers de Bretagne
Gendarmes Bourguinons/Gendarmes d'Anjou
Gendarmes de Flandres/Chevaulégers d'Anjou
Gendarmes de la Reine/Gendarmes de Berry
Chevaulégers de la Reine/Chevaulégers de Berry
Gendarmes du Dauphin/Gendarmes d'Orléans
Chevaulégers du Dauphin/Chevaulégers d'Orléans
Beausobre Hussars (4 squadrons)
Lynden Hussars (4 squadrons)
Artillery Train – Prince d'Eu
8 12lb Field Pieces
6 8lb Field Pieces
36 4lb Field Pieces 'Ordinaires'
50 4lb Field Pieces 'à la Suédoise'

THE PRAGMATIC ARMY – WILLIAM AUGUSTUS, DUKE OF CUMBERLAND & CAPTAIN-GENERAL

BRITISH CONTINGENT

FOOT GUARDS – LIEUTENANT-GENERAL WILLIAM ANNE, EARL OF ALBEMARLE

Guards Brigade – Brigadier Robert Carpenter
1st Foot Guards (Grenadier Guards)
3rd Foot Guards (Scots Guards)
2nd Foot Guards (Coldstream Guards)

FOOT – LIEUTENANT-GENERAL SIR JOHN LIGONIER

Royal Brigade – Major-General Henry Ponsonby/Brigadier George Churchill
Royal Scots (1st Foot)
Royal North British Fusiliers (21st Foot)
Handasyde's (31st Foot)
Duroure's (12th Foot)
Onslow's Brigade – Major-General Henry Pulteney/Brigadier Richard Ingoldsby
Onslow's (8th Foot)
Rothes (25th Foot)
Johnson's (33rd Foot)
Howard's (19th Foot)
Howard's Brigade – Major-General Charles Howard/Brigadier Henry Skelton
Howard's (3rd Foot)
Royal Welch Fusiliers (23rd Foot)
Skelton's (32nd Foot)
Pulteney's (13th Foot)
Sowle's Brigade – Major-General John Campbell of Mamore/Brigadier Thomas Bligh
Sowle's (11th Foot)
Bragg's (28th Foot)
Cholmondley's (34th Foot)
Bligh's (20th Foot)
Artillery supporting the Brigades of Foot
17 3lb Field Pieces
6 1½lb Field Pieces

HORSE – LIEUTENANT-GENERAL SIR JAMES CAMPBELL

First Line – Earl of Rothes' Brigade
Hawley's Dragoons (3 squadrons)
Bland's Dragoons (3 squadrons)
First Line – Bland's Brigade
3rd Troop, Horse Guards
4th Troop, Horse Guards
2nd Troop, Horse Grenadiers
Earl of Hertford's (3 squadrons)
Second Line – St Clair's Brigade
Honeywood's (3 squadrons)
Ligonier's (2 squadrons)
Second Line – Onslow's Brigade
Campbell's Dragoons (3 squadrons)
Stair's Dragoons (3 squadrons)

ARTILLERY TRAIN – COLONEL JONATHAN LEWIS

10 6lb Field Pieces
10 3lb Field Pieces
4 8in. Howitzers

HANOVERIAN CONTINGENT – GENERALLEUTNANT THOMAS EBERHARD VON ILTEN

First Line – Brigade von Böselager
Böselager (1 battalion)
Oberg (1 battalion)
Campe (1 battalion)
Second Line – Brigade von Zastrow
Zastrow (1 battalion)
Spörcken (1 battalion)
First Line – Brigade de Launay
d'Acerre (2 squadrons)
Leibgarde (2 squadrons)
Wendt Dragoners (4 squadrons)
Second Line – Brigade von Montigny
Dachenhausen (2 squadrons)
Montigny (2 squadrons)
Aldersleben Dragoners (4 squadrons)
Artillery Train
12 3lb Field Pieces

DUTCH CONTINGENT – KARL AUGUST, FÜRST VON WALDECK-PYRMONT

FOOT

First Line – Brigade Stürler
Cronström (Dutch)
Bentinck (German)
Salis (Swiss) (2 battalions)
First Line – Brigade Elias
Rijssel (Dutch converged grenadiers)
Oranje Stad en Lande (Dutch)
Oranje Vriesland (Dutch)
Buddenbroek (Dutch)
First Line – Brigade Salis
Schaumburg-Lippe (German)
Ayla (Dutch)
Gardes te Voet (Dutch)
Second Line – Brigade Efferen
Dorth (Dutch converged grenadiers)
Constant-Rebecque (Swiss) (3 battalions)
Second Line – Brigade Burmania
Stürler (Swiss) (2 battalions)
Broekhuizen (Dutch)
Second Line – Brigade Halkett
Bronckhorst (Dutch)
Smissaert (Walloon)

CAVALRY

First Line – Brigade Vrybergen
Rechteren-Overijssel (3 squadrons)
Buys (1 squadron)
Sandouville (3 squadrons)
First Line – Brigade Schagen
Hopp (2 squadrons)
Nassau-Ouwerkerke (1 squadron)
Carabiniers (3 squadrons)
Garde Dragonders (5 squadrons)
Second Line – Brigade van Oyen
Lijnen (3 squadrons)
Schack (3 squadrons)
Ginkel (3 squadrons)
Second Line – Brigade van Schlippenbach
Hessen-Homburg (3 squadrons)
Nassau Dragoons (4 squadrons)
Artillery Train
6 6lb Field Pieces
24 3lb Field Pieces
4 Howitzer

RESERVE CORPS – FELDMARSCHALLEUTNANT VON MOLTKE

Ligne Dragoners (Austrian) (2 squadrons)
Styrum Dragoners (Austrian) (2 squadrons)
Karóly Hussars (Austrian) (2 squadrons)
Belézny Hussars (Austrian) (2 squadrons)
Freikompagnie Bouvier (Austrian)
Freikompagnie Pertuiseaux (Austrian)
Sempill (British) (1 battalion)
Cope's Dragoons (British) (3 squadrons)
Waldeck (Dutch) (1 battalion)
Schlippenbach Drag. (Dutch) (7 squadrons)

OPPOSING PLANS

THE ALLIES

From the outset of the campaign, the Allies suffered from two crucial disadvantages compared with the enemy. Firstly, the seeming air of complacency which had led to the delays in appointing Wade's successor literally left the appointee at sea on board a Royal Navy squadron heading for The Hague, whilst secondly, Saxe's decision to commence operations earlier than the norm meant that the Allied commanders would be forced into a reactive strategy, necessitating that they respond to French movements rather than implement their own strategy.

As initial, confused, reports began to arrive in Brussels, the absence of the Captain-General meant that the army was headless, being governed by consensus rather than policy, and thus, while measures were agreed and undertaken to concentrate the field army at Anderlecht, just outside Brussels, this was the limit of what was and could be done.

Upon his arrival, Cumberland was faced with one of two choices. He could either implement a plan of his own devising, in the hope that in doing

Although regarded as the last time that a British monarch was personally to lead his troops in battle, King George II courted dissent and controversy at the battle of Dettingen by wearing the uniform and insignia of a Hanoverian general officer rather than that of a British officer. This would be one of several unresolved issues that would still be felt at Fontenoy two years later.

Pistol made in London by the English gunsmith John Harman. Previously a member of the London Gunmakers' Company, Harman was later to establish his own premises and in 1729 was appointed gunmaker to Frederick Louis, the Prince of Wales. Backed by this royal patronage he produced some of the finest bespoke firearms of the period, a number of which are in the Royal Collection. (Image reproduced with kind permission of the Musée d'Histoire militaire de la Ville de Tournai)

so he could force Saxe to abandon his own plan of campaign, or he could attempt to thwart the enemy from achieving his own objectives, once they became clear. The problem with the former was that, should he give Saxe 'free rein' to act as he pleased, he would be placing a great and perhaps prohibitive strain upon the alliance as both Vienna and The Hague would no doubt view a marauding French Army in the dimmest possible light.

The assembly of the army at Anderlecht had been an eminently sensible decision from both a military and political standpoint as, from this central position, Cumberland would not only be able to cover the centre of government but, sitting astride the principal lines of communication, he would also be able to quickly evaluate incoming reports of enemy activity and act upon them accordingly.

During the previous councils of war, Sir John Ligonier – as senior British officer – and the Prince of Waldeck, commanding the Dutch, had both argued that the army should move to engage the enemy as soon as was practicable, whilst Königsegg – the Austrian commander, and theoretically Cumberland's deputy – had argued that the best course would be to hold the present position and await reinforcements, some of which were on the way and some of which could be drawn from garrisons. The responsibility naturally now devolved upon Cumberland, and after consideration he decided that the Army would march to engage the enemy at Mons, where the most recent reports had placed Saxe and his army. The reasons why he chose to take this, the riskier option, are several:

Firstly, all available information pointed to the fact that Saxe had taken the field with no more than 30,000 men and Cumberland was simply unable to divorce himself from the belief that – as things stood – his own forces comfortably outnumbered the enemy, and, even if there was an error in these estimations, it was not believed to be a critical factor.

Secondly, the more time that went by without the Allies engaging the French Army, the greater the chance that Saxe would be able to achieve his objectives. Additionally, and if, as it seemed, Saxe was intent on the capture of Mons, few senior officers believed that the garrison would put up much of a fight and were therefore loath to hand the enemy a strategic victory through simple inactivity.

Thirdly – and this was a purely British perspective – Cumberland and his senior officers, as veterans of Dettingen, simply could not conceive of their being defeated by the French under what they perceived to be the prevalent conditions for the current campaign. Two years earlier, the French had trapped the Allied Army on the banks of the Main and, ignoring the fact that a French blocking force under the Duc de Grammont had abandoned its positions in order to attack them, concentrated their appreciation of the battle on the superlative performance of the British infantry who repulsed one enemy attack after another and then shattered Grammont's troops, opening a route to safety before the rest of the French Army could come up.

Finally, and perhaps most importantly, the Allies believed that Saxe's condition was indeed terminal and that, with his death, news of which was expected on a daily basis, the strategic direction would go out of the enemy campaign. As a result, the belief was that when the armies eventually met on the field of battle, the French would be commanded by his, undoubtedly less able, successor.

The plan of campaign was therefore a simple one. The army would march to Mons to engage and defeat the French besieging forces, and, once the threat to the Austrian Netherlands had been resolved, the Allies would have the option of conducting offensive operations or redeploying to await the previously mentioned reinforcements.

As a result, although the Allies were fairly quickly disabused of the notion that Mons was the principal French objective and that Saxe's target was in fact Tournai, it was not until the evening of 9–10 May that they actually knew where the battle would be fought and, given the inadequate reconnaissance, Cumberland never really understood that the Pragmatic Army would really be engaging only the enemy right flank rather than the whole body. As such, his deployment and plan of battle were more of a 'textbook' nature than anything else – the Anglo-Hanoverians, organized during the march into a single 'wing', would take the 'post of honour' on the right of the army, and the other wing, consisting of the Dutch contingent, would take the left. The Austrians, bolstered by detachments from the rest of the army, would form a general reserve.

The plan was simple in itself; the Dutch were to drive upon the village of Fontenoy and the ridge above the Chemin de Condé, cutting the French line in two and then driving into the French rear, behind Antoing, before striking for the bridge at Calonne and cutting their line of retreat. The Anglo-Hanoverians, for their part, would simply advance up the Chemin de Mons, using firepower to sweep any enemy aside and continue advancing until they overran the enemy centre before redeploying to meet any new threat. Should the Dutch fail in their objectives, it was believed that they would at least be able to keep the enemy engaged for long enough to allow the redcoats to achieve theirs and win the battle. The only amendment made to this was the creation of an independent brigade under Brigadier Richard Ingoldsby for the purpose of clearing the Bois de Barry and seizing the Redoute de Chambonas in order to protect the Anglo-Hanoverian right flank.

THE FRENCH

The central pillars of Saxe's plan of campaign for the summer of 1745 were misinformation and timing, the former in that he needed to keep Cumberland in the dark about his actual objectives for as long as possible and the latter to ensure that the various strands of his plan came together at exactly the right time. The only way to do this was to make certain that he was 'seen' by the enemy, forcing the Allies to commit themselves to a course of action which became redundant almost as soon as it was adopted and as such – at least until the armies came to within striking distance of each other – he always remained one step ahead of his opponent.

In his military writings, Saxe had postulated that choice of ground and suitable preparation could nullify an enemy's numerical advantage and, believing that he would ultimately be outnumbered by the Pragmatic Army, his primary aim was therefore to lure the enemy to a battlefield of his choice, and to do this he needed to bait the trap by threatening a target that the Allies could not ignore, in this case by choosing the fortress of Tournai.

Saxe's strategic plan – the Austrian Netherlands, May 1745

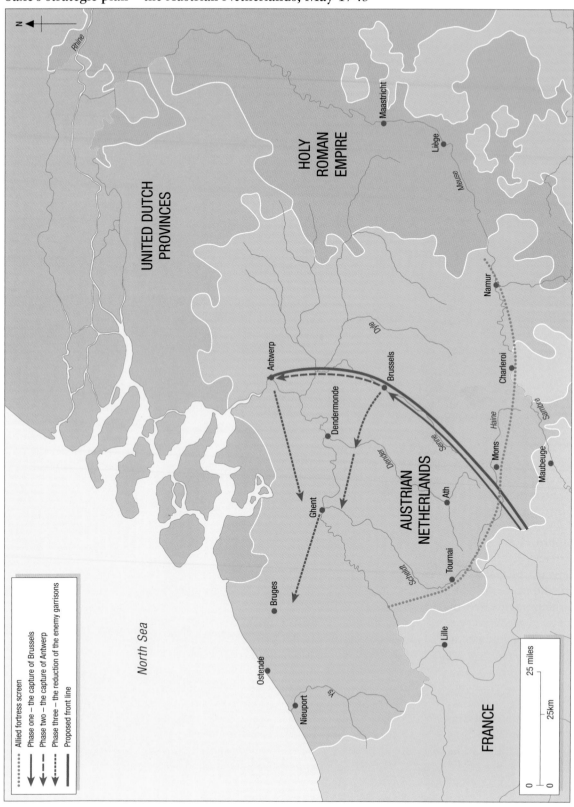

Given the necessity to find a favourable defensive position, the next phase was to supply the enemy with misinformation about his actual objectives, which in the event worked perfectly, drawing the Allied Army firstly in the direction of Mons and then – once Cumberland had realized his error – towards Tournai. But these were simply the means to an end. If Cumberland, at any stage, failed to take the bait, then the strategic gains – albeit the capture of one of the barrier fortresses – would be negligible in comparison with the aim that Saxe had set himself, namely the destruction of the Pragmatic Army as a viable fighting force, the overrunning of the western part of the Austrian Netherlands, and the capture of Brussels as a springboard towards the capture of the whole province.

The flaw in Saxe's concept was that as a major road hub there were naturally several routes all leading to Tournai, and once he had settled upon the area around Fontenoy as his chosen battlefield, these would all need to be covered to ward against any unwelcome surprises, thus necessitating a division of the army in the face of the enemy.

To cover for these eventualities, Saxe divided his army into four components: with the main body, now divided into two wings, marching off to take up position around Fontenoy, Brézé would remain in command of the besieging forces at Tournai, whilst a detachment of two brigades of infantry and two of cavalry under Löwendahl was deployed to cover the eastern approaches to the city – this latter force being close enough to support both the field army and the besieging force in their activities.

Saxe's battle plan relied upon the enemy throwing themselves upon a series of prepared positions supported by carefully sited artillery, when, at the crucial moment, he would launch a counterattack and break them. As such, the two wings would be unequal in size, this being a reflection of their tasks. The left flank, under the Comte de Bérenger, had but two infantry brigades and a small number of cavalry to cover the approach from Leuze, a road which he felt would be most unlikely for the Allies to use in any great strength. The right flank, under the Marquis de Lutteaux, was separated from Bérenger by the northern part of the Bois de Barry, and consisted of the rest of the army with the exception of the cavalry reserve and the troops of the Maison du Roi. Lutteaux's instructions were to cover the southern approaches to Tournai, and his forces were deployed in a fish-hook, which stretched from the banks of the Scheldt near the town of Antoing, southwards towards Fontenoy and then northwards across the face of the village towards the Bois de Barry, the line being punctuated by a series of artillery redoubts which augmented the field defences that had been hurriedly thrown up around Fontenoy itself.

This would mean that when the two armies finally engaged in combat on 11 May, Cumberland would be making plans to attack only part – albeit the largest part – of the French Army, whilst Saxe was forced to withhold committing the detachments under Bérenger and Löwendahl to the battle for fear that, by ordering them to the threatened sector, he would compromise his whole plan of campaign. As such, the reactive strategy that he had forced upon the Allies in order to bring them to his chosen battlefield had now given them the initiative. All that Saxe could do now was to wait for the opening moves of the enemy attack, trusting that his deployment of troops would be sufficient to contain them for long enough to enable him to bring all available troops to bear and then to crush them in a counterattack.

THE CAMPAIGN

OPENING MOVES

On 13 April 1745, Saxe gave orders for the Army of Flanders to begin offensive operations. The main body was to assemble at Maubeuge, with Valenciennes and Warneton acting as mustering points for the troops from Northern France (including the Maison du Roi) and Flanders respectively. Five days later, following an emergency medical operation, he set out to take personal command of the units at Maubeuge, totalling 37 battalions of infantry and 25 squadrons of cavalry. Command of the forces at Warneton (16 battalions and eight squadrons) was given to the Marquis de Brézé, whilst the Vicomte du Chayla was appointed to lead the line units (nine battalions and 22 squadrons) marching from Valenciennes.

French siege mortar. At Tournai, the Marquis de Brézé – commanding the French besiegers – was to prosecute the siege with 25 12lb and 20 8lb 3oz mortars, together with 90 heavy cannon with calibres ranging from 12lb to 33lb. The interesting thing to note is that the mortars fired a smaller projectile than their listed calibre, thus the 12lb mortar fired a round which was 11lb 8oz and the smaller weapon an 8lb round. (Image copyright and reproduced with kind permission of the Musée d'Histoire militaire de la Ville de Tournai)

Having decided upon Tournai as his objective, the first thing that Saxe had to do was to convince the enemy that his target was elsewhere, and thus a detachment under the Comte d'Estrées was given instructions to feint towards Charleroi and Mons, drawing the enemy's attention upon himself, before occupying a blocking position at St Ghislain – west of Mons – which he reached on 24 April, being joined shortly afterwards by Chayla's column.

Having set the wheels in motion, Saxe now led the troops at Maubeuge westwards, away from his supposed objective, and then northwards, heading towards Tournai, crossing the Haine, just as Estrées was appearing in the vicinity of Mons. With the weather deteriorating, Saxe was forced to halt his troops for two days at Péruwelz, and, frustrated by this enforced inactivity and aware that time was slowly turning against him, he detached a picked force of 6,000 men under the Duc d'Harcourt, with orders to make the best possible speed to Tournai and seal off the eastern approaches to the city; in addition a courier was sent to Chayla ordering him to pull back to Leuze and block the road between Ath and Tournai.

At Warneton, and as the main body of the army conducted its campaign of misinformation to the south, Brézé prepared for his pivotal role in the operation – the masking of the left bank of the Scheldt around Tournai and the effective opening of the siege, upon which so much depended. Screened by the bad weather he moved to within four miles (6½km) of his objective and, during the early hours of 26 April, iron jaws closed shut around

the city as the two French columns advanced under the cover of a thick fog, cutting Tournai off from the outside world and bringing the first phase of Saxe's plan to a successful close.

Two days later, Saxe's men moved into the siege lines, crossing over to the left bank of the Scheldt, from where he planned to make his primary effort, directing his artillery against the same sector of walls breached by Marlborough during the siege of 1709. Once the troops were in place, orders were given for the engineers to construct pontoon bridges across the river at Constantin and Calonne in order to facilitate communication and movement between both banks.

His plans maturing as intended, Saxe now sent orders to Estrées, ordering him to abandon all pretence that Mons was a campaign objective and to retire upon the main army.

Reminiscent of his study of Napoleon after the battle of Laon in 1814, this painting by Jean-Louis Ernest Meissonier shows a hard-riding Saxe at the head of his staff. At Fontenoy, and in deference to his severe ill health, King Louis XV gave Saxe permission to travel by carriage and, when he eventually mounted his horse to direct the battle, he was exempted from having to dismount in the Royal presence.

BRUSSELS

As the wheels of Saxe's plan turned and gathered momentum, the situation in the Allied camp was one of disarray. Although, in Cumberland's absence, orders had gone out for the concentration of the army at Anderlecht, it was still a state of affairs at complete variance with the agreement with the civilian government that in the absence of the Captain-General: '[t]he Army would be assembled quickly in order that an offensive campaign could

The armies move to battle

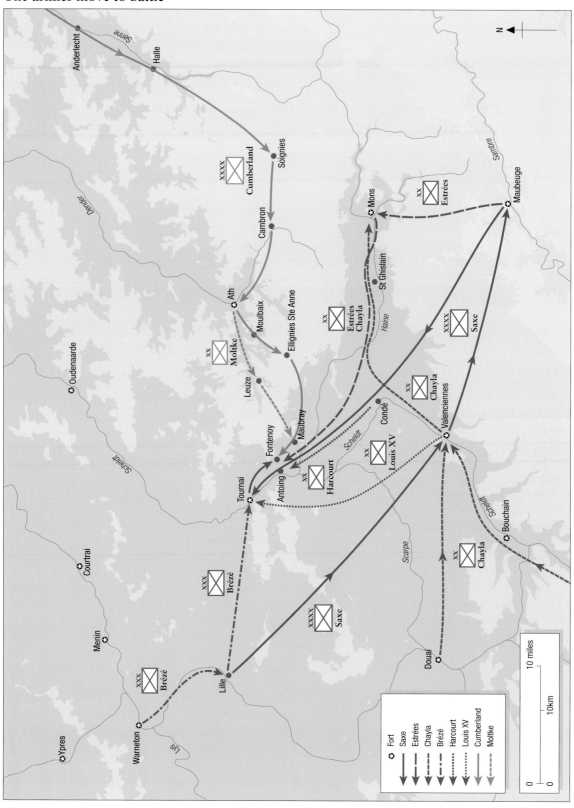

LEFT
One of Cumberland's 'Beloved Brothers' this reconstruction shows the uniform and equipment of a British infantryman of the 1745 campaign, the dark blue facings being indicative that the regiment in question has a royal connection. At Fontenoy, these regiments would have been the three battalions of Guards, the Royal Scots and Royal North British Fusiliers (both in the 'Royal' brigade) and the Royal Welch Fusiliers (Howard's brigade). (Image copyright and reproduced with kind permission of Gabriele Mendella)

RIGHT
Famed through the literature of Alexandre Dumas, the Mousquetaires du Roi formed an integral part of the Royal Guard, the Maison du Roi, and were organized into two companies, known by the colour of their horses – either 'black' or 'grey'. This reconstruction is of the uniform of a member of the 2nd Company as he would have been in dismounted order during the 1745 campaign. (Image copyright and reproduced with kind permission of Gabriele Mendella)

be opened at the earliest possible opportunity in order to cover the Dutch Provinces, and that to bring the Army up to full strength, drafts would be taken from various garrisons'.

Opinion was divided in that, whilst the Austrians counselled that the barrier fortresses be allowed to do their job of holding up the enemy whilst the Allies built up their forces for a decisive battle, the British and the Dutch advocated an aggressive forward defence, supporting their case with the 'intelligence' that Saxe commanded a mere 30,000 men at Maubeuge – they would attack the French in overwhelming numbers and, having captured the enemy magazine, use it as a springboard for further operations.

The arguments went to and fro for a crucial week, with the Austrian position no doubt being undermined by departure of the bulk of their forces in Flanders for service against the Prussians in Silesia, and then the news from Count van Nava, in command of the fortress at Mons, that a significant enemy force had driven in his outposts and that a formal siege was only a matter of time.

The news arrived in Brussels at the same time as Cumberland and, with Mons by now undoubtedly under siege, the task was obvious, and orders given for the army of almost 53,000 men (21,000 British, 8,000 Hanoverians, 22,000 Dutch and 2,000 Austrians) to march south in order to break the siege. But in the interim, more and ever-contradictory reports were coming in from the French border – Saxe had left Maubeuge and was now besieging Mons; Saxe had abandoned the siege of Mons and marched elsewhere, destination unknown; a French army had appeared at Leuze, between Ath and Tournai, threatening both fortresses – the rumours persisted and grew, and the Allied position remained dangerously unclear. Even when irrefutable news was received of the investment of Tournai, the Allied commanders believed that this was yet another diversion and that the true danger would still come from the south. But the following day these opinions changed and the relief of the city on the Scheldt now became the Army's objective.

Cavalry sword, Mousquetaires du Roi. Less ornate than the Walloon-style weapons carried by many of the Maison du Roi this Musketeer's weapon displays a distinctive triangular cross-section near the hilt, which flattens out as it tapers towards its point. (Image copyright and reproduced with kind permission of the Musée d'Histoire militaire de la Ville de Tournai)

At a final council of war, Cumberland decided that the best way to support the beleaguered garrison would be to move against Saxe's lines of communication and supply, which he erroneously believed were still being traced from Maubeuge, and then to move north, bringing the enemy to battle before the walls of Tournai where the French commander would be forced to divert a significant part of his forces to maintaining the siege in order to prevent a sally taking his army in the rear. Confident that he held a marked numerical superiority, Cumberland ordered the troops to march out on 30 April, heading initially towards Mons, where the main army and any reinforcements gathered along the way would reorganize themselves for the decisive encounter.

In the light of the heavy criticism of his handling of the campaign Cumberland would later reflect:

I confess that had I have known that the Dutch defence of Tournai would not have been conducted in the same plaintive manner as the defence of several other fortresses in the previous campaign I would have been better served to have held off from an immediate attack and allowed the enemy to waste his resources by throwing his men against the defences … but our decisions were dictated by the belief that the town would fall quickly unless relieved.

As the troops left Anderlecht, the weather turned for the worse, the columns being drenched by sheets of torrential rain and, despite the efforts of pioneers ranging in front of the army to prepare the way ahead, the road soon became a quagmire, slowing their progress considerably.

The first day's march saw the bedraggled columns reach Halle some 10 miles (16km) from Brussels, where a rest day was declared to allow the men to dry out from the driving rain, and it was here that Cumberland dictated the structure of the army, assigning the Anglo-Hanoverians and Dutch to the right and left wings respectively, whilst using the Austrian contingent as the core of an army reserve. On 2 May the army pressed on to Soignies, but disaster struck when it was found that the Dutch quartermasters had made insufficient provision for their troops, and Cumberland was once more forced to halt the advance whilst wagons were sent to Mons to collect the requisite supplies.

The Allies remained at Soignies for two more days before continuing to Cambron – on the road between Ath and Mons – where they halted for a further five days to allow stragglers, including the bulk of the transport and artillery, to catch up with the main body. With the wagons from Mons came the news that French 'besiegers' had melted away, destination unknown and for the first time since assuming personal command of the army, Cumberland felt that he had concrete evidence about where his enemy was – before Tournai.

From Cambron, the most direct route to Tournai – via Leuze – was reported to be held by the enemy, and so Cumberland sent the Austrian Lt. Gen. von Moltke at the head of a flying column to test the accuracy of this intelligence, and for once it proved to be correct, Moltke running headlong into Chayla, who had been placed there to cover exactly such an eventuality. After a desultory skirmish the French retired but remained in loose contact, leaving the Allies in possession of the town and regretfully secure in the knowledge that the broken terrain to the west precluded an advance along this axis.

For Cumberland, the only positive aspect of the encounter at Leuze was that Saxe would experience the same risks working in the opposite direction, and so in effect the Allies' right flank was screened. What this meant, however, was that the only viable approach routes to Tournai lay to either the north-east or the south-east of the city, the problem being that the former option would entail the army moving back along its line of march, along muddy, churned-up roads, leading to inevitable delays. In effect, he had only one option and so, instructing Moltke to re-join the main body, he gave orders for the march to continue westwards to Moulbaix, where, after heavy skirmishing with French outposts, the army concentrated on the afternoon of 8 May.

Therefore, and in the end, Cumberland had been forced to act exactly as his enemy had calculated, playing directly into his opponents' hands, and, whilst the English duke was a relative newcomer to the soldier's trade, Saxe, in comparison, was a tried veteran and would not squander the gift that he had been given. The ignorance about the enemy's intentions is best summed up in the Duke's own words to the Earl of Harrington:

> For my own part I cannot believe that the enemy will wait for us, notwithstanding it is assured that the French King is at Lille, if not at the army. My reasons are that they might have disputed our passage hither with great advantage of ground: that they have withdrawn their baggage across the Schelde, and not thrown up earth to form a circumvallation. However I cannot say that everyone is of my opinion that the enemy will retire. I cannot come *to any* certain knowledge of the enemy's numbers, but I have concurring information that the body on this side of the Schelde does not exceed 31 battalions and 32 squadrons.

It is clear from the above that, even at this stage, Cumberland still believed Saxe's campaign of misinformation and the deficiency of his own intelligence reports, that all he needed to do would be to continue his resolute advance and the enemy would fall back before him, ultimately abandoning the siege of Tournai and crowning a successful campaign.

French infantry officer's sword. (Image reproduced with kind permission of the Musée d'Histoire militaire de la Ville de Tournai)

LEFT
Often known as a 'Charleville' musket after one of the principal armouries where it was produced, this .69-calibre, 1728-pattern musket was the most common French firearm of the 18th century. Improvements on the earlier 1717 model included an iron ramrod and a new barrel assembly, which allowed for easier maintenance. Over 375,000 weapons of this type were produced before the introduction of the 1763 model. (Image copyright and reproduced with kind permission of the Musée d'Histoire militaire de la Ville de Tournai)

RIGHT
Lock detail of a British Long Land Pattern Musket – the famed 'Brown Bess'. This .75-calibre weapon was the mainstay of the British infantry from 1722 until 1838, and was accurate to about 170 yards (155m), although British doctrine relied on volley fire at about a third of that distance. (Image reproduced with kind permission of the Musée d'Histoire militaire de la Ville de Tournai)

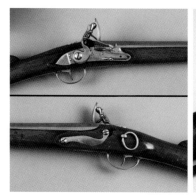

TOURNAI

Whilst the Allies made their meandering way towards Tournai, Saxe began to make his final dispositions for the field action that he sought. Having reinforced Brézé with three cavalry regiments that had recently arrived in camp and nine battalions of militia from Lille and Douai, he now intended to take the field with the remainder of the Army of Flanders, together with the Maison du Roi and the Brigade des Gardes upon their arrival.

The decision now was where to fight the defensive battle, and Saxe mentally began to narrow down the various options: firstly, the Allies could approach from the north, along the road from Oudenaarde, but he quickly disregarded this option as the route was bordered in the west by the Scheldt and dominated to the east by the Mont St Trinité, from where his artillery could decimate the enemy before they could close for battle. To the east, the route from Ath via Leuze was the most direct but bad going for cavalry and favouring a defence in depth – Cumberland would indeed be foolish to send his entire force by this road, but it would still need to be covered. The third option lay to the south-east, where the Chemin de Mons passed through a narrow gap bordered by the Scheldt and the Bois de Barry. The terrain was perfect for his purposes with a ridgeline running south-east from the Scheldt at Antoing before eventually turning eastwards at Fontenoy in the direction of the Bois de Barry. A defensive line here would be securely anchored on both flanks, and the Saxon had more than enough manpower to improve upon what nature had provided. In addition, the ground north of the ridge – whilst under crops and sodden by the recent rains – was eminently suitable for the deployment of a large body of cavalry.

Basing his decision on what he saw to be an over-exaggerated reliance on the part of the Allies to keep an open and unhindered line of communication with Brussels, the French Marshal mentally discounted the first two options, drafting tentative plans for fighting an engagement south of Tournai, but, ever the strategist, he accepted the fact that his decision might be wrong and made arrangements for both of the other approaches to be sufficiently covered by troops. With no detailed intelligence about Cumberland's position, Saxe's tentative plans remained exactly that, but then, following the combat at Leuze on 7 May, he now received the information that he urgently needed and committed himself to battle.

Collection of various musket balls taken from the battlefield; note the irregular shape of many of them. (Image reproduced with kind permission of the Musée d'Histoire militaire de la Ville de Tournai)

On the morning of 8 May, the *boute-selle* was sounded in the cavalry encampment at Cysoing and the troops ordered to move southwards towards Antoing, whilst the field artillery were given instructions to cross over the bridgehead at Calonne, prior to moving south. The Comte de Löwendahl was given an independent command consisting of two cavalry and two infantry brigades, and given orders to occupy the area around the Mont St Trinité, whilst the Comte de la Vauguyon, commander of the Brigade du Dauphin was ordered to march down to the village of Fontenoy which stood at the centre of the proposed battle line and place it in a state of defensive readiness. Detailing 450 men to begin the construction of almost a mile (1,600m) of defensive works, Vauguyon then set parties to loopholing buildings and clearing fields of fire. Incorporating the stone churchyard wall into their defences, the French eventually screened all but the northern face of the village with a manned trench line, the spill from which was then used to build a number of artillery positions and an earth rampart, which would be defended by a second line of troops. With these measures under way, Saxe then sent a courier to King Louis XV to advise him that a battle was likely.

In order to finalize his dispositions, Saxe sent his Chief of Staff – the Marquis de Crémilles – to conduct a detailed reconnaissance of the deployment area, and, whilst Crémilles was fulfilling his task, he was advised of the presence of a body of enemy troops in the vicinity: Moltke's detachment making their way from Leuze to Maubray. On receiving the news, Saxe gave orders that only those infantry units which were to deploy in the line from Antoing to the Bois de Barry were to move forward into position, temporarily holding the remainder back as a reserve.

The Royal Bodyguard – the Garde du Corps – formed the oldest element of the Maison du Roi, and comprised truly the elite of the elite French cavalry. Organized into four companies (one nominally Scots and three French), this reconstruction represents the uniform of the Third French Company, which was commanded at Fontenoy by Francois, Duc d'Harcourt. (Image copyright and reproduced with kind permission of Gabriele Mendella)

Although woodland has now encroached upon the terrain, the ridgeline towards the right of the image marks the French positions between Antoing and Fontenoy.

Memorial to the Marquis de Talleyrand and those men of the Régiment de Normandie who were killed in the explosion at Tournai on 9 May and their comrades who fell at Fontenoy two days later, whilst in action against the British 'Brigade of Guards'.

Wanting the enemy to commit themselves to an attack and thereafter make it difficult for them to disengage, it was obvious therefore, that the French deployment could in no way seem overly daunting to the Allies; Saxe needed to bait the trap and make sure that Cumberland walked into it. Dividing his army into three unequal forces, Saxe assigned the bulk of his front-line troops to the Marquis de Lutteaux who with eight infantry brigades would hold the line from Ramecroix southwards to Antoing. To Lutteaux's left the Comte de Bérenger commanded two infantry brigades watching the Chemin de Leuze; the reason for this imbalance being that Saxe was now certain that the main Allied attack would come up against his left flank, and he wanted a single officer in command of the sector, thus giving stability to the line. Behind these ranks of bayonets, two lines of cavalry were able to give support where required. It was now that Saxe gave instructions for the construction of a number of artillery redoubts to bolster the front line and ensure that, at whatever point the enemy attacked, they would be caught in an artillery crossfire.

That night Saxe slept fitfully. He had done everything in his power to bring the enemy to battle, but the problem remained whether Cumberland was either brave enough or confident enough to take up the gauntlet that had been thrown at his feet, something that the Allied commander had so far shown no sign of doing, but he was also still concerned about the king, uncertain about the malign influence of his enemies at court. Until now he seemingly had his sovereign's trust and confidence but had this been compromised and his authority eroded? For the Protestant soldier of fortune, it was a conundrum to which he would only have the answer when the king spoke the following morning. Which would carry the greater weight? His religion, his nationality or bastardy or his undoubted military ability? In the end he need not have worried, for King Louis XV, either through humility or the knowledge of his own limitations defused any potential confrontation by stating that whilst at Versailles his word was law, on this battlefield he was just one more soldier under Saxe's command: 'Gentlemen, I have entrusted the Marshal with the command of my Army, and it is my wish that his orders

Saxe's proposed dispositions, midday 9 May 1745

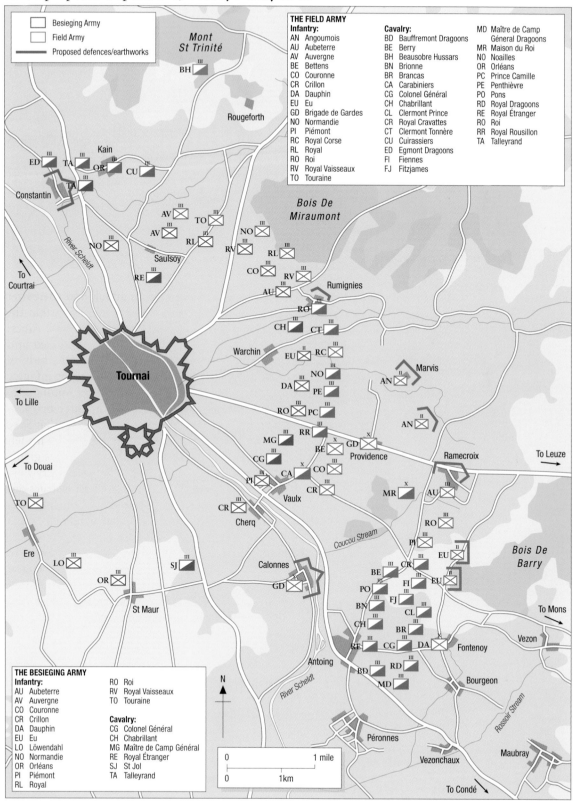

Legend:
- ☐ Besieging Army
- ☐ Field Army
- ▬ Proposed defences/earthworks

THE FIELD ARMY

Infantry:
AN	Angoumois
AU	Aubeterre
AV	Auvergne
BE	Bettens
CO	Couronne
CR	Crillon
DA	Dauphin
EU	Eu
GD	Brigade de Gardes
NO	Normandie
PI	Piémont
RC	Royal Corse
RL	Royal
RO	Roi
RV	Royal Vaisseaux
TO	Touraine

Cavalry:
BD	Bauffremont Dragoons
BE	Berry
BH	Beausobre Hussars
BN	Brionne
BR	Brancas
CA	Carabiniers
CG	Colonel Général
CH	Chabrillant
CL	Clermont Prince
CR	Royal Cravattes
CT	Clermont Tonnère
CU	Cuirassiers
ED	Egmont Dragoons
FI	Fiennes
FJ	Fitzjames

MD	Maître de Camp Géneral Dragoons
MR	Maison du Roi
NO	Noailles
OR	Orléans
PC	Prince Camille
PE	Penthièvre
PO	Pons
RD	Royal Dragoons
RE	Royal Étranger
RO	Roi
RR	Royal Rousillon
TA	Talleyrand

THE BESIEGING ARMY

Infantry:
AU	Aubeterre
AV	Auvergne
CO	Couronne
CR	Crillon
DA	Dauphin
EU	Eu
LO	Löwendahl
NO	Normandie
OR	Orléans
PI	Piémont
RL	Royal

RO	Roi
RV	Royal Vaisseaux
TO	Touraine

Cavalry:
CG	Colonel Général
CH	Chabrillant
MG	Maître de Camp Général
RE	Royal Étranger
SJ	St Jol
TA	Talleyrand

Scale:
0 — 1 mile
0 — 1km

N ↑

35

Begun in 1907, and paid for from subscriptions by the Irish Literary Society, this Celtic cross was erected in the town square of Fontenoy to commemorate the actions of the Irish Brigade. Constructed from stone quarried in Ireland, the granite cross stands upon a marble pediment and is inscribed in both French and Irish. The *cense* or fortified farmhouse in the background would have been used as the headquarters of the Marquis de Lutteaux.

be followed by all without exception. Here, it is he who holds the command, and I shall be the first to set an example by submitting myself to his orders.'

It was a sentiment echoed by the newly arrived Duc de Noailles, Saxe's former sponsor, who, despite being the senior officer, likewise vowed to serve in whatever function the Marshal felt he would be best suited. Saxe looked at both men with gratitude, the former his adopted sovereign and the latter, not only a soldier and statesman of great repute, but a blood relative of many of his enemies at court, few of whom would now risk royal or familial disfavour.

DEPLOYMENT FOR BATTLE

Given the various detachments he had been forced to make, Saxe approached the coming battle at a numerical disadvantage, albeit confident that if the anticipated threats failed to materialize, he would be able to recall both Bérenger and Löwendahl before the fighting began in earnest. Predicated upon the reasonable assumption that the British contingent of the Pragmatic Army would occupy the 'post of honour' on the right of the Allied attack, Saxe decided to maintain a defence in depth with which to absorb and then repulse Cumberland's assault; for the French commander the equation was simple – the Austrians, Dutch or Hanoverians simply needed to be held, but the British, in order to play upon the political opposition to the war, needed to be comprehensively broken.

Fortified and covered by a series of entrenchments, Antoing was held by the Brigade Piémont, supported by two batteries each of six 12lb cannon, in addition to which a further battery of six heavy pieces, originally intended for the siege lines at Tournai, was deployed on the opposite bank of the Scheldt in order to be able to enfilade any Allied attacks on the town. The line from Antoing to Fontenoy was held by the Crillon and Bettens brigades, the line punctuated by three artillery redoubts containing a total of 16 cannon and supported by three regiments of dragoons in dismounted order – Mâitre de Camp, Royal and Beauffremont.

Held by the Dauphin Brigade, whose members now packed the defensive works and, supported by the Régiment du Roi, Fontenoy was the key to the French position, the front line itself was continued by the Aubeterre brigade, under the Marquis d'Anlezy, which was still awaiting the arrival of its supporting artillery. Flanking Aubeterre, and occupying the position upon which Saxe felt the main enemy blow would fall, stood the Brigade des Gardes (four battalions of the Gardes Françaises and two of the Gardes Suisses supported by four cannon) at the head of which stood the Duc de Grammont, Noailles's nephew and one of Saxe's most vocal critics. It could be argued that the Gardes had been placed here not only in acknowledgement of their prestige within the army, but also because the commander-in-chief was relying on their desire to redeem themselves after their disastrous showing at Dettingen two years earlier. Directly behind the Gardes Suisses, the three battalions of the Royal Vaisseaux (with four guns) under the Comte de Guerchy stood astride the Chemin de Mons, at that time the sole tactical reserve available.

Aligned with the Swiss guards, the Prince de Soubise commanded the Brigade d'Eu, whose named regiment occupied two redoubts on the edge of the Bois de Barry (the Redoute d'Eu and the Redoute de Chambonas), whilst the woods themselves were occupied by the Arquebusiers de Grassin, an independent unit which had been thrown forward to contest any Allied attempt to flank the French positions. Completing the infantry deployment, and likewise deployed in support of Soubise, stood the famed Irish Brigade, six battalions of Wild Geese under the command of the Comte de Thomond, supported by the eight battalions of the Couronne and Royal brigades.

Immediately behind the infantry, and under the command of the Comte d'Eu, Saxe deployed his 60 squadrons of line cavalry in two unequal lines.

A popular image, this watercolour depicts Saxe directing the battle from his wicker carriage. In reality, and despite critical ill health, he spent almost nine hours in the saddle.

In the first, from left to right, the Royal Rousillon and Prince Camille regiments – led by the Marquis de Clermont-Tonnere – took station to the north of the Chemin de Mons, whilst to the south of the road, the line continued with the brigades of Royal Cravattes, Clermont-Prince and Colonel-Général the eight regiments coming under the command of the Duc d'Harcourt. The second, smaller line of horsemen commanded by the Vicomte du Chayla marshalled the brigades of Berry, Noailles, Brionne and Royal Étranger, occupying a position directly behind Harcourt's right flank.

Farther to the rear, Saxe diplomatically placed King Louis and his entourage near the hamlet of Nôtre Dame au Bois, from where his sovereign could observe the progress of the battle and satisfy his martial ardour, whilst remaining in a position of relative safety from where – in the event of a disaster – the royal party could be quickly rushed across the Scheldt bridgeheads and into Brézé's siege lines at Tournai. Naturally where the king was, so was the Maison du Roi, and these elite troops together with the Brigade de Carabiniers formed the core of the army's mounted reserve, taking up position behind, but some distance to the rear of Clermont-Tonnere's two regiments of horse.

By nightfall on 10 May, Saxe's plans had almost come to fruition; the army had been deployed with great care, both with regard to terrain and arcs of fire, whilst elsewhere the siege of Tournai was proceeding exactly as he had intended. All that he needed was for the enemy to be drawn into attacking, and, as the royal suite retired for the evening, Saxe remained with his troops, presumably sleeping at Lutteaux's headquarters, in order to ensure that whatever the Allies had planned for the following day, he would be more than ready.

MAUBRAY AND WASMES

On the evening of 9 May amidst yet another torrential downpour, Cumberland gave orders that, the following morning, an operation would be mounted to clear the enemy outposts lying athwart the Allied line of advance; each Wing

Cumberland's proposed plan of attack, 10–11 May 1745

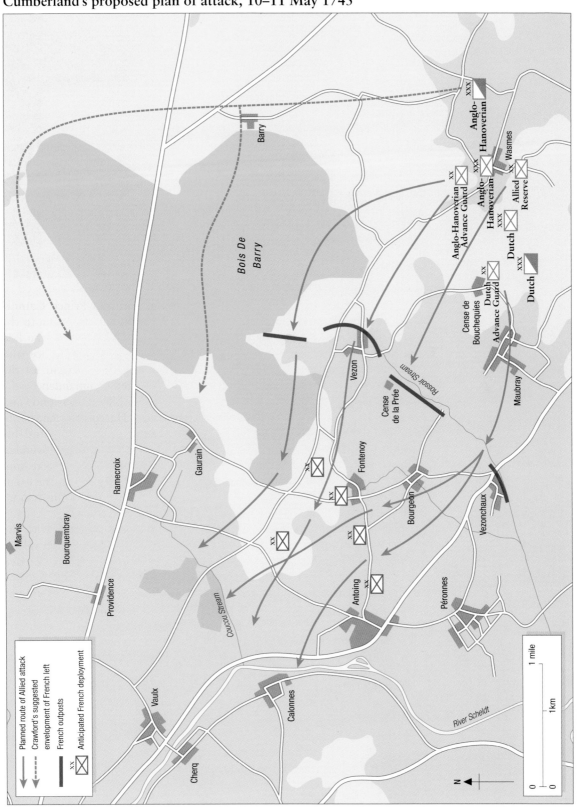

Barry

Bois De Barry

Anglo-Hanoverian

Anglo-Hanoverian

Wasmes

Anglo-Hanoverian Advance Guard

Allied Reserve

Dutch

Cense de Bouchequies

Dutch Advance Guard

Dutch

Vezon

Rossoit Stream

Cense de la Prée

Maubray

Ramecroix

Gaurain

Fontenoy

Bourgeon

Vezonchaux

Marvis

Bourquembray

Péronnes

Providence

Coucou Stream

Antoing

Vaulx

Calonnes

River Scheldt

Cherq

Planned route of Allied attack

Crawford's suggested envelopment of French left

French outposts

Anticipated French deployment

1 mile

1 km

N

would form a detachment of eight battalions of infantry and 12 squadrons of cavalry to which would be added all available grenadier companies, six cannon, two howitzers and 500 pioneers, with the Reserve Corps deploying in order to support either column as circumstances dictated. All told, some 18,000 men – almost one-third of the army – were now detailed to take part in the operation to clear no more than a few hundred Frenchmen from the line of advance. It was a case of the Allies using a sledgehammer to crack a walnut.

The sodden ground made for difficult going and as such the troops were late in stepping off, but in the face of such overwhelming numbers the French *piquets* were easily swept aside, however, when the Dutch cavalry pushed too far forward they triggered several rounds of long-range enemy artillery fire, and were sent scurrying back into cover. As a result, and whilst the Anglo-Hanoverians were constricted by terrain, the Dutch were later, under the cover of darkness, to shift their axis of advance somewhat farther west thereby establishing the Allied forward positions along the line Péronnes–Bourgeon–Vezon.

At his field headquarters in Vezon, Sir James Campbell – in command of the British part of the clearing operation – had by now received a number of reports to the effect that the French had occupied the Bois de Barry in strength, and diligently passed this information up the chain of command, recommending that the woodland be cleared before the advance continued, as failure to do so would open the army to a flank attack. Politely acknowledging Campbell's report – but signally failing to act on it – Cumberland now decided to reconnoitre the French position himself and, as the Allied generals and their staffs rode forward, many of them now began to understand the full nature of the conundrum with which Saxe had presented them.

It was soon clear that, hampered by the muddy ground, this would be no conventional, linear, battle; it would be one in which the terrain and the enemy's position would combine, as time progressed, to gradually force the Allied wings apart from each other, preventing Cumberland from fully co-ordinating their actions. This would give rise to the danger that each wing would have to fight its own individual battle against an entrenched opponent operating with the joint advantages of a smaller frontage and interior lines, factors which would enable Saxe to react to the ebb and flow of battle far quicker than they could themselves. Secondly, it was certain that a commander of Saxe's calibre would have sited his artillery to its best advantage whilst the French deployment itself had served to nullify the Allied cavalry, reducing their effectiveness to one of two options: either to exploit an Allied breakthrough or – the unthinkable – to cover an Allied retreat. It was a deadly puzzle with no easy solution.

At this point, and with the majority of those present pressing for a general engagement, the Earl of Crawford, one of Campbell's brigadiers, requested that the right wing be extended northwards through the woods, not to clear them but rather to outflank the French line. There was a pregnant pause as he looked to his colleagues for support, but none came and then, no doubt imagining overwhelming numbers of Frenchmen hiding in the trees, Cumberland closed the matter, denying the Scotsman's request. For the second time that day, the Captain-General chose to ignore or discount the opinions of an experienced subordinate; decisions which would have a marked effect on the development of his battle plan and the conduct of the Anglo-Hanoverian forces.

For Cumberland, it had now all come down to two final options – either to give battle on ground of the enemy's choosing or to manoeuvre further and attempt to regain the tactical advantage. He himself was in favour of an attack, and perhaps he was steered to this opinion by the presence of King Louis and the Dauphin with the French Army – the capture of one or the other would be a valuable pawn in the diplomatic chess which would follow an inevitable Allied victory.

Gradually the discussions drew to a close, with Cumberland giving instructions: 'Tomorrow at 2 a.m. the whole army will move to the position which the detachments occupy to-day, and will form in order of battle in the manner which the generals shall find the most suitable, having regard to the ground over which they may have to manoeuvre. After which the army will march on the enemy.'

In effect, the Dutch would engage the French positions overlooking the Chemin de Condé, with their extreme right flank moving against the village of Fontenoy itself, whilst the Anglo-Hanoverians, moving up the Chemin de Mons, would drive through the French line between Fontenoy and the Bois de Barry, indirectly supporting the Dutch attacks by splitting the French Army in two. Once these primary objectives had been achieved, the right wing would continue to engage the main body of the enemy army whilst the Dutch would cut their line of retreat by seizing the bridgehead over the Scheldt at Calonne.

In his own account of the campaign, Waldeck would later insist that the initial Allied attack failed as a result of the lack of cohesion between the two wings, stating that the Anglo-Hanoverians were not advanced far enough to offer the support that Cumberland had intimated his troops would receive, citing this as the principal reason for the failure to carry Fontenoy by assault. Given that this ideal proximity would have required the redcoats to deploy almost directly under the barrels of the French artillery, the truth is more likely that Waldeck ultimately compromised his own attack by advancing farther than had been previously agreed with the army commander.

That night, for once, the army slept under clear skies, and as the troops 'stood to' in the early hours of 11 May, Moltke was given instructions to send both *Freikompagnien* into the Bois de Barry to provide flank security for the Anglo-Hanoverian advance.

Marching in four columns – the Dutch infantry and cavalry under Cronström and Coenders respectively, with the Anglo-Hanoverian foot under Ligonier and horse under Campbell and Wendt – the Allies were concealed by the early morning twilight and a heavy mist that settled on the ground (an unlooked-for advantage that ultimately proved to be a double-edged sword as the men stumbled across the ditches, orchards and fields, their progress being further hampered by their commanders' inability to gauge distances accurately). Crossing

A direct contemporary of John Harman, the French gunsmith Gilles Massin of Liège made firearms for the French royalty and nobility. This pistol would have been the possession of one of the more affluent officers of the French Army. (Image copyright and reproduced with kind permission of the Musée d'Histoire militaire de la Ville de Tournai)

The second component of the French Brigade des Gardes, this reconstruction shows the uniform of a private or *fantassin* of one of the two battalions present at Fontenoy. (Image copyright and reproduced with kind permission of Gabriele Mendella)

more open terrain, the Dutch made better progress but, on the right, Vezon was a bottleneck that could be negotiated by only a single brigade at a time. Thus when the Guards Brigade, on the extreme right, finally reached its allotted position, the 1st Foot Guards took post on the right of the brigade line, while the 2nd Foot Guards needed to wheel, counter-march and then wheel again in order to take their station on the left of the brigade line, and finally the 3rd Foot Guards would manoeuvre in a similar fashion to take their position in the centre of the line.

In the darkness, Moltke's flanking companies had by now come into contact with the men of the Grassins and, after a heavy exchange of fire, he committed the Dutch Waldeck regiment to flank the Frenchmen, who retired with slight loss. Hearing of the encounter, and undoubtedly regretting that he had failed to act upon Campbell's previous intelligence, Cumberland now ordered the creation of an ad hoc brigade, the task of which would be to sweep the enemy aside and secure the woods for the Allies. Withdrawing Duroure's and Pulteney's British regiments from their parent formations and rounding off the brigade by the addition of both Böselager's Hanoverians and Sempill's highlanders from the reserve, he gave the command to Richard Ingoldsby, a Guards officer with whom he was well acquainted, currently serving as brigadier of Onslow's brigade.

At 4.00am the Captain-General mounted his horse and with a small escort rode along the front of the army and, satisfied that all was well, drew up in front of Colonel Jonathan Lewis of the train ordering him to fire four blank rounds from the 6lb 'flag gun', the signal for the army to advance.

PÉRONNES AND BOURGEON

Having captured the village of Bourgeon the previous evening, Waldeck now had the luxury of being able to deploy his men in a fairly open area, the downside to this being that they would be attacking the longest portion of the enemy line, a position studded with fieldworks, with relatively little artillery support. If that were not bad enough, he was obliged to make this attack leading a force in which, with the possible exception of the Guards and Swiss regiments, he had little personal faith. His opinion of his subordinate officers was little better, believing that the majority were political cyphers, merely serving their time in the field before moving on to appointments elsewhere.

Waldeck's advance was led by the bulk of the Dutch cavalry, whose task was to secure Péronnes and then act as a screen for the left flank of the infantry, who, marching behind them in two 'divisions', would halt parallel to their objectives and then, by simply wheeling right, be in a position to launch their attack, the intention being that the first 'division' would hit the southern face of the village and, pivoting on its right flank, lap around it to the west, whilst the second 'division' would attack the area between Antoing and Fontenoy and prevent the enemy forces here from supporting the village.

The first of many problems to be faced by the Dutch that morning was that the firing of the 'flag gun' had completely thrown away the element of surprise and the French gunners, their cannon having been sited the day before, simply needed to open fire, scoring several hits and causing the Dutch cavalry to scatter.

With their initial objective achieved, Waldeck now ordered Prince Ludwig von Hessen-Phillipsthal's three brigades of cavalry to move onto the plain between Antoing and Péronnes in order to screen the advancing infantry, who by now had wheeled north and were marching towards the enemy lines. Each division was directly supported by 12 3lb cannon and some howitzers, and, with the exception of Waldeck's own regiment which was with the Reserve, these were the sum of the Dutch infantry – there were no reserve battalions either to commit in the event of success or to fall back upon in the event of failure and so, given the size of the opposing forces in this sector, it is doubtful that Waldeck had even considered an attack on Antoing, preferring instead to mask it with cavalry.

The Chemin de Mons looking north from Vezon to the ridgeline. The Anglo-Hanoverians would have advanced directly towards the site of the factory on the upper right section of the image.

Making their way gradually forward, the Dutchman and his troops slowly came under sporadic fire from the enemy guns, making them more than grateful for the protection afforded by the early morning mist. But the protection would be fleeting as every man present knew that in time it would burn off and, when it did so, they would find themselves in plain view of an entrenched enemy, committed to attacking across fields devoid of defensive cover.

It is unclear whether, at this point, Waldeck was aware of the decision to delay the advance of the right wing and take the time to clear the Bois de Barry, but what is clear is that the Dutch objectives were limited in scope – in his journal, he naturally cites the village of Fontenoy and also what he refers to as the 'Redoutes d'Anthoin', obviously referring to the earthworks above the Chemin de Condé. The town of Antoing itself, was never really a feasible objective; he simply did not have enough infantry available to attack all three places at once with any reasonable chance of success – and even the chances of attaining the two objectives Waldeck quotes were really only realistic if the French line could be hit at several points simultaneously. In other words, if the Anglo-Hanoverians could engage the eastern face of the village at the same time, something they were unable to do.

At 5.00am, and with the sun yet to rise in the east, a Dutch battery at Vezonchaux signalled the formal beginning of the battle by opening fire upon the village of Fontenoy. In the semi-darkness, the effect of the guns was less than negligible, serving only to trigger a further enemy response, their muzzle flashes giving their location away to the French artillery.

VEZON

The unexpected cannon fire – ineffective as it was – alerted Cumberland to the fact that soon his troops would need to deploy under heavy enemy fire and so he summoned his senior commanders to another meeting to reassess the situation. In the interim, and as his small force disengaged from contact,

Moltke sent a runner to the army headquarters, advising Cumberland of the discovery of an enemy redoubt on the far edge of the wood, perfectly sited to enfilade Ligonier's brigades as they advanced.

Despite Campbell's earlier misgivings, and indeed despite the sporadic artillery fire which echoed across the battlefield, it seemed as if no real urgency had been attached to Ingoldsby's mission and it was only after 6.00am that he began his advance towards the Bois de Barry, intent on using a sunken cattle track as cover from enemy fire for his approach. But now, seeing movement along the tree line – the woods having been re-occupied by the Grassins – and fearful of being outnumbered, he halted the column some distance short of its objective, sending back a request for artillery support, which soon arrived in the form of Captain Mitchelson of the Royal Artillery commanding three 6lb cannon.

The mist was by now beginning to disperse and, as the enemy slowly came into view, the French gunners on the ridgeline began to open fire upon the massed British foot. Fearing that his prized infantry would be flayed by the enemy cannon, Cumberland dispatched an aide to Sir James Campbell ordering that the first-line cavalry move in front of Ligonier's troops to screen them from the enemy guns as they continued their deployment. Summoning two of his brigadiers, the Earls of Rothes and of Crawford, Campbell related Cumberland's instructions, deliberately elaborating his explanation somewhat in anticipation that in the meantime Ingoldsby would have succeeded in his mission and secured the Bois de Barry.

With no sounds of combat coming from the nearby forest, and with the advancing infantry battalions now pushing up against each other on the Chemin de Mons, Campbell sent one of his aides-de-camps – Captain John Forbes of Stair's dragoons – to find out what Ingoldsby's situation was. On being told that further progress was impossible without the arrival of the requested artillery support, Forbes rode back to the cavalry commander to relay the unwelcome information.

Northward-facing view from the positions of the Gardes Françaises towards the Bois de Barry. The battalions of the Irish Brigade would have been initially deployed facing eastwards along the tree line.

By now the enemy cannonade had become more general and, as the French batteries to their front rained down fire around the village of Vezon, Campbell realized that he could delay no longer and reluctantly ordered the advance. Within minutes, an enemy round shot had crashed into the midst of the leading horsemen and Campbell was thrown to the ground with his leg in tatters. After some rudimentary battlefield surgery he was carried from the field on an improvised litter, but the shock and extent of the injuries proved to be fatal and the command passed to his deputy, Lt. Gen. Henry Hawley, who was farther down the line of march and still needed to be informed of the circumstances of his accession to the senior command. Although the regiments of the first line were now technically leaderless, it should again be stressed that they were not without orders and that experienced officers such as Crawford and Rothes were more than capable of following the instructions they had been given but, behind the dispersed line of horsemen, the red-coated infantry were now stacked up along the roadway and, despite the enemy artillery fire, Ligonier was obliged to order the leading battalions to march through Vezon and deploy for action.

Having received the requested artillery support, it was only now that Ingoldsby began to follow Cumberland's orders. With the cannon using grapeshot to drive the enemy back from the edge of the wood, he ordered Colonel Scipio Duroure's battalion, supported by Pulteney's and Sempill's regiments, to assault the French position at bayonet point, but Mitchelson's fire had had little effect, and a series of concentrated volleys from the Grassins, who had by now resumed their earlier positions, sent the redcoats reeling back in disorder. The presence of the British guns now prompted a reaction from the Redoute de Chambonas and the three cannon were quickly redeployed to engage in counterbattery fire. Naturally this served to relieve the pressure on the Grassins who resumed their harassing fire from the cover of the trees. His troops going to ground once more, Ingoldsby sent Captain Crawford of Pulteney's regiment to Vezon for further instructions, and it

Interior view of the Bois du Barry clearly showing its use as 'managed' woodland and dispelling the myth of its impenetrable nature. Had Ingoldsby been more aggressive in his advance, he would have, in all likelihood, secured his objective forcing Saxe to commit his reserves to its recapture.

was now that the first signs of Cumberland's being out of his depth began to appear with his exasperation at the brigadier's apparent inability to fulfil even the simplest of orders.

Reporting back, Crawford told Ingoldsby he was to 'defend himself if attacked, but by all means to seek out and attack the enemy'. A different account was later given by Major Balfour of the Royal Artillery who stated that he had clearly heard Cumberland tell Crawford that the brigadier was to 'attack the battery in the wood, and maintain himself if he could; and if not to make the best of his way off'. And yet another version of what was said comes from Captain Joseph Yorke of the 2nd Foot Guards, who reported that the Duke's instructions were simply 'Let him go and attack as fast as he can!'

Whichever of these three versions is the most accurate, it is clear that the situation was deteriorating steadily and Cumberland urgently needed to get a grip on things as the Allied attack was in danger of spiralling out of control before it had really begun. As the debate over Ingoldsby's orders continued, a courier arrived from Ligonier asking for artillery to be brought up to silence the French guns and, after giving orders for the remaining seven 6lb cannon to move forward, he ordered Captain, the Viscount Bury, to ride to Ingoldsby and ascertain his situation in person.

On the firing line and by this stage seemingly unable to issue coherent orders, Ingoldsby was transfixed, preferring the perceived shelter of his current position to the danger of running the gauntlet of enemy fire. This was how Bury found him, demanding to know – in the Duke's name – what was happening and what his immediate intentions were. The shaken officer stammered 'that he saw troops in the wood, that he did not know the numbers of them and that having consulted with his officers, all were of the opinion that further attack was impracticable'. Given the later conduct of two of these officers during the second attack on Fontenoy, this last is possibly debatable. Turning his horse, Bury galloped off to report to the commander-in-chief, who, in a thunderous mood, now rode to confront his errant subordinate in person.

View from the French positions above the Chemin de Condé showing the Dutch start positions as viewed from the deployment areas of the Bettens and Crillon brigades. Devoid of cover, the attacking troops were caught in a murderous crossfire as they advanced towards their objective.

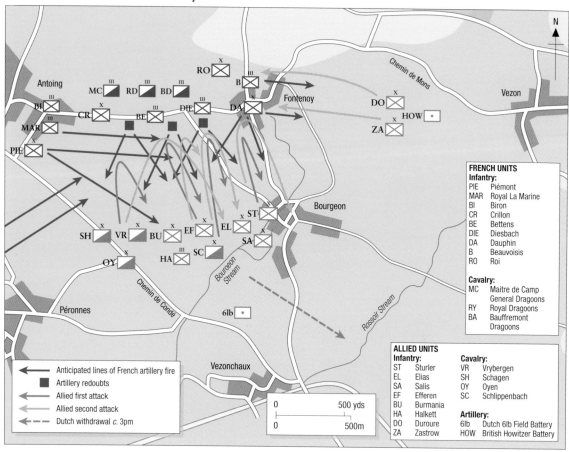

With head bowed, Ingoldsby stood silent as Cumberland, looking down from his excited mount, poured a torrent of colourful invective over his head, making it not only clear what he thought of the brigade's inactivity but also explicitly informing its commander what would happen should his command not obey the Captain-General's next orders and obey them with the utmost alacrity.

THE DUTCH ATTACK

After two hours of largely inconclusive fire, the guns around Fontenoy began to fall silent as cannon were cooled down and ammunition supplies replenished, and against this backdrop Waldeck gave orders for the Dutch brigades to attack the village, the blue-coated infantry advancing steadily, beginning to echelon towards their target points – Cronström's division, supported by the flanking cavalry, moving towards the line of redoubts whilst Waldeck's own command headed towards the village.

Within Fontenoy itself, the men of the Dauphin Brigade stood to behind the recently constructed defences, a forward line of musketeers occupying the fire trench which formed the first line of defences with a second line of troops poised to man the earthen rampart behind them, once the enemy had closed

This view of Fontenoy Church, in the early morning mist, is exactly as it would have appeared to Waldeck's attacking troops.

and the artillery had ceased firing. To the rear, supporting companies were arrayed either behind a series of barricades or in the loopholed buildings, ready to add their fire to repulse the enemy. The battalions were deployed conventionally with the first battalion of the Dauphin Regiment on the right of the line, followed by the second and third, with the Beauvoisis Regiment closing the left flank of the brigade as it covered the Chemin de Mons. The most crucial sector of the line – a circular bulwark enclosing the village church and graveyard – was held by the brigade's converged grenadier companies. The defences were completed by a total of eight 4lb cannon which were attached to the brigade, and a number of guns drawn from the artillery reserve, deployed as ad hoc batteries at strategic points around the perimeter defences.

With a perfect view of the developing attack, the Marquis de Lutteaux was more than content to allow the enemy to close to point-blank range before giving the order to open fire. Uncharacteristically, the French deployment would allow almost every musket to be brought to bear, whilst his cannon would be able to engage the enemy until almost the last possible moment. Contrary to this, the Dutch needed to close the gap and come into hand-to-hand combat as soon as possible, which meant that their supporting artillery had only a limited window of opportunity to engage the defenders before the danger of hitting their own troops made further fire prohibitive.

Riding to the front of his division, Waldeck drew his sword and pointed it at the French positions and, with drums beating, the Dutch foot began their stately advance towards their objective. To their left, Cronström's regiments followed suit and, as they did so, Waldeck sent one of his aides – Lt. Col. Francois Cornabé – to the Swede, reiterating his instructions that he press the attack between Antoing and Fontenoy, i.e. against the line of redoubts, in order that the Dutch cavalry reserve would gain the room to manoeuvre and be in a position to exploit the anticipated breach in the enemy defences.

Advancing steadily the Dutch battalions slowly closed with the enemy, but if Waldeck was later to criticize the British for not being close enough to support his attack, it should be noted that his own command had started off far closer to their objective than Cronström's, which naturally meant that there was virtually no chance of both forces striking the enemy line simultaneously. Then, as the lines of infantry came to within effective musket range, a cry of '*Vive le roi!*' echoed from the French. Within moments the walls and barricades around Fontenoy became enshrouded with gun smoke as the defenders' muskets and cannon erupted with fire, scything holes in the ranks of the attackers. Taking this as their cue, the remaining French gunners opened fire, the lines of enfilade – the 'Swedish Cross' – that Saxe had so carefully calculated, devastating the Dutch ranks, smashing into them from both front and flank and then, almost as a leisurely afterthought, the heavy cannon deployed on the far side of the Scheldt now began to engage Cronström's infantry by taking them in the rear.

The effect was electric with the attack on the redoubts coming to a crashing halt and the Dutchmen going to ground in a vain attempt to find cover where there was none, exposed to the relentless enemy cannonade, their disorder being so complete as many troops massed together that Cronström would later be unjustly accused of attempting to form his battalions into square in the face of the enemy cannon fire.

Casimir van Schlippenbach, a Dutch cavalry brigadier was particularly scathing of the infantry when he wrote, '[they] remained inactive, allowing themselves to be subjected to the hail of cannonballs rather than to make even the slightest attempt to carry on the attack'.

Yet his own arm of service was not excluded from the debacle as, when the cannon balls began to fall into their ranks, Hessen-Phillipsthal's cavalry scattered for a second time and, although the majority of the troops were eventually brought into order, a number of officers and men fled the field, reputedly bringing news of the Allied defeat to the garrison of Ath before the army had been fully engaged.

Further testimony to the confusion on the extreme Allied left comes from Lt. Gen. Hobbe, Baron van Aylva who wrote: 'I saw whole regiments which, despite all previous signs of steadfastness and bravery, nonetheless remained immobile, without direction, as if immobilised by fear... And others whose actions are nothing but shameful, notably a colonel and a major who rode from the battlefield at the head of two squadrons, no doubt fleeing for Mons or Brussels'.

A soldier's perspective of the early morning battlefield. This panorama clearly shows how the battlefield would have looked to men from both sides, their view obscured by a heavy mist that burned off before the Allied left wing could reach its objectives.

Around Fontenoy itself, Waldeck's battalions had by now closed with the enemy and were engaged in a desperate fight to break into the village but unsupported, and, in order to prevent his being counterattacked on his, by now open, flank he threw his second line into the attack so that his men were fully engaged against the 'hook' of the French line, although with Cronström seemingly unable or unwilling to advance farther he was now isolated and success had to come quickly or not at all.

It is at this point that the first of many contradictions enters into the accounts of the battle as some sources cite that the leading elements of Ilten's Hanoverian brigades led

THE VILLAGE OF FONTENOY, APPROXIMATELY 8.00AM, TUESDAY 11 MAY 1745 (PP. 50–51)

Moving into the village on the afternoon of 8 May, the Comte de la Vauguyon – in command of the Brigade du Dauphin – immediately began to place Fontenoy in a state of defence when, over the next two days, his troops constructed almost a mile (1.6km) of defensive works (1): the outer approaches were covered by a shallow trench, filled with debris, to disrupt an enemy attack; then a fire trench which would be manned and form the first physical line of defence; then, slightly raised, and constructed mainly from the earthen spill of the forward trenches, manned by both infantry and artillery, with the final line of defence being a series of loopholed houses and barricaded streets.

Having been alerted by the early morning exchange between the French and Dutch cannon, the fire trench has already been manned and, as the enemy slowly materialize from the early morning twilight, the French gunners begin to prepare their light 4lb pieces for action (2). Their stores of powder and shot being held in a cottage that has been stripped of all flammable material, an officer makes sure that there are sufficient supplies for a period of sustained fire.

Standing at the rampart, and viewing the Dutch advance through a borrowed telescope, Marshal Saxe (3) is seen giving the Marquis de Lutteaux – commanding the French right wing – his final instructions for the battle to come, knowing that he will shortly be required elsewhere and trusting in his subordinate's ability to beat off the Allied attack. Behind them, their grooms stand ready with their horses and, as soon as the meeting is over, Saxe will ride for his battlefield headquarters escorted by a number of troopers on detached duty from the Volontiers de Saxe.

Away from the rampart, Vauguyon can be seen addressing a party of senior regimental officers (4) whilst two companies of Dauphin are standing in readiness for when the guns are withdrawn and they are ordered forward to man the rampart and provide the second line of defence.

To the west, one of the three artillery redoubts constructed to cover the French line overlooking the Chemin de Condé can be seen, manned by the red-coated Swiss of the Brigade de Bettens (5) which forms the first link in the chain joining Fontenoy with Antoing.

Beyond the French position, the Dutch line can be seen making its steady advance, at the moment covered by the light mist, which is starting to disperse. From left to right come firstly, Waldeck's division (6), including the famed Gardes te Voet, heading towards Fontenoy itself, and beside them Cronström's division (7), the task of which will be to engage the French position above the Chemin de Condé and prevent the enemy troops from being able to offer support or reinforcement to the village. North of Cronström are Hessen-Phillipsthal's cavalry brigades (8) which have been given the unenviable task of screening the infantry from enemy fire, and beyond them – held in reserve – Coenders' cavalry, tasked with exploiting the anticipated breakthrough.

With the Allies marching into a crossfire, the attack will become a shambles in less than half an hour.

This painting of Fontenoy by Louis Nicolas van Blarenberghe shows the Allies (left centre) marching steadily into the crucible of combat. To the left of the image, near the two pillars, King Louis XV and his entourage observe the progress of the battle. (Galerie de Batailles, Palace of Versailles)

by their converged grenadiers, now attacked the farther end of the village, engaging the Beauvoisis Regiment and one of the battalions of Brigade du Roi. The problem with this contention is that the Hanoverians were still to the rear of the right wing and thus were unlikely to be in a position to go into action that early. The likelihood is that these commentators have merged the two Dutch attacks into a single event.

Whatever the truth of the Hanoverian intervention it would have been insufficient to delay the collapse of the Dutch attack, as later described by one of Waldeck's officers: 'our approaching troops were so received by the French infantry that they fell completely into chaos and were thrown back and it was only with numerous threats that we were able to bring even a small number back into some semblance of order'.

Waldeck had no other option than to order the retreat. His own troops needed time to re-form before they would be of further use in the battle, whilst Cronström's battalions were caught in a deadly crossfire which would result only in their complete and utter destruction should they not be pulled back into cover. Reluctantly giving the necessary orders, he quickly penned a note to Cumberland, assuring him that – with support – he would attack once more, as soon as his forces had had a chance to reorganize themselves.

Irrespective of on whose shoulders any blame should fall for uncoordinated assault on the French positions, it is abundantly clear from these words that the Dutch attack had indeed collapsed, and that Saxe's battle plan had passed its first serious test.

LIGONIER

As more of his infantry arrived on the battlefield, Sir John Ligonier was faced with a dilemma. Earlier, when the cavalry under Campbell had deployed to his front, it had been to screen his men from the enemy artillery, thereby saving them for the planned attack, and yet he now needed to advance his first line of troops in order that the second could form up, yet the space was still occupied by the horsemen. There were but two choices open to him:

either the cavalry needed to move closer to the enemy, placing them within effective range of the French 4lb batteries, or they needed to pull back behind the infantry, with any resulting casualties being accepted as a necessary evil.

Accordingly, he sent an aide-de-camp to Hawley, suggesting that the mounted screen be withdrawn in order to allow the foot to complete their deployment. At the same time he sent another officer to Cumberland himself, requesting that the remaining seven 6lb guns be brought forward to engage the French batteries and sweep them from the ridge, adding that until this was accomplished a frontal attack – should it be ordered – would be more or less unfeasible.

It was now a little after 9.00am and Ligonier's message came at one of those decisive moments upon which the outcome of the battle would hinge. For several hours the Anglo-Hanoverian forces had continued their deployment – a process which was still far from complete – whilst the intended manoeuvre designed to secure the Bois de Barry had yet to take place. Coupled with this, Cumberland was now having to digest the unappetizing news that Waldeck's initial attack had been repulsed with loss. With the British infantry brigades slowly filing into position it was now approaching the moment of decision, when Cumberland would need to choose between either attack or withdrawal – Saxe's defensive posture clearly precluded a rapid pursuit in the event of an Allied disengagement, therefore and perhaps for the last time during the battle, the initiative rested firmly with the Pragmatic Army. The battle was still for Cumberland to win, or lose.

For the moment the Captain-General was still certain that his original plan continued to be a viable one; after all, British fire drill was a tried and tested formula that had won many a battle and it must be said that a leavening of British redcoats would surely stiffen the faltering Dutch and thus ensure the capture of Fontenoy, whilst his earlier intervention had – he felt – undoubtedly cured Ingoldsby's indecision.

He was wrong, and it was inevitable that any further news that the brigade had still yet to move a single step in an attempt to secure his objective would re-ignite his fury, and once again Cumberland abandoned the responsibilities of an army commander, removing himself from the chain of command at a time when his presence and ability to issue orders was of paramount importance.

Ignoring Ingoldsby's excuses, Cumberland summoned the lieutenant-colonel in command of Böselager's Hanoverians, ordering him in German to advance and carry the enemy redoubt at the point of the bayonet. But before this potentially suicidal attack could take place, he changed his mind and, finally losing patience with his former favourite, effectively abandoned the plan to clear the woods once and for all, ordering Duroure's and Sempill's battalions to make themselves ready to move in support of a fresh Dutch attack on Fontenoy.

Even as this last exchange was taking place, the hapless Ingoldsby was hit by an enemy musket ball and carried to the rear, command of his reduced brigade now devolving upon the Hanoverian Maj. Gen. Ludwig von Zastrow, who led the remaining two regiments to fall in alongside Sowle's brigade in the British second line.

Deployed behind the infantry brigades were a total of 29 3lb cannon for close support, but as these would be deployed only after Ligonier's

command had crested the ridge ahead, it was natural that his request for artillery support to suppress the French guns be addressed, hence the request for Lewis's guns to be brought forward. Normal practice was that during the march they would be hauled by civilian contractors and handed over to the military when they deployed for battle. In combat, the guns would be manhandled by infantrymen and commanded by artillerymen. At Fontenoy, the sodden sloping ground and muddied ploughed fields would require them to be dragged using rope and tackle; no doubt this gave rise to the later belief that Cumberland's civilian contractors had deserted the army upon receipt of their pay – another ground later given for the failure of the Allied plan – yet, as civilians, they were not required to take position in or near the firing line, rather instead they were to remain in the rear of the army until their services were required again.

Halting his deployment, Ligonier made space for Lewis's guns to move to the front and around 10.30am they were ready for action – seven pieces in the main battery with Mitchelson's detachment of three guns still engaging the Redoute de Chambonas from their position near the Bois de Barry. It was not long before the heavier British pieces began to have an effect, the first major casualty being the Duc de Grammont, commander of the Gardes Françaises, whose legs were shattered when his horse was struck by a cannonball. Slowly but steadily Lewis's men began to silence the French guns and, on the ridgeline, it was clear that the unequal contest would have but one outcome and, as the Marquis de Brocard, Saxe's artillery commander, rode forward to oversee the redeployment of one of the batteries before it succumbed to the Allied cannonade, he too was struck down, arguably a greater loss to the French Army than Grammont had been.

Ligonier's first line was now complete. Taking the 'post of honour' on the extreme right of the line was the Guards Brigade, commanded by Brigadier Robert Carpenter of the 3rd Guards. Next in seniority came the Royal Brigade under Maj. Gen. Henry Ponsonby, Onslow's brigade, led by Maj. Gen. Henry Pulteney completing the formation. Immediately behind them, and slowly deploying from right to left, the second line consisted of the brigades of Maj. Gen. Sir Charles Howard, and Sowle's, under Maj. Gen. John Campbell of Mamore. Adjacent to Campbell's battalions stood Thomas Eberhard von Ilten with the remainder of the Hanoverian Brigade. Ilten was another general who today would seek to lay to rest the ghosts of Dettingen – for the British he was 'His Majesty's Confectioner General', a scathing lampoon upon his conduct during that battle where he had allegedly kept his troops out of the line of fire allowing the French artillery to bombard the British, who were trying to fight their way to safety. Later, when asked for an explanation he had simply replied '*J'ai préservé les troupes de sa Majesté*' and the British satirists had naturally latched onto the similarity to the English word 'preserve' – a fruit jam.

A PLAN UNFOLDS

Unlike his counterpart, Saxe had chosen not to spend the evening before the battle in relative comfort, but instead spent the night sleeping on the front line, seeking no concessions to his ill health. Thus it was, in the early morning darkness, when the Dutch artillery opened fire, that he was able to react quickly and judge for himself whether or not his plans would need to be refined as changing circumstances dictated.

As the sun rose, he could easily make out the Allied deployments, secure in the knowledge that he had chosen his blocking position well, that the Dutch would be attacking arguably the weaker sector of the French line whilst the Anglo-Hanoverians would engage where he was strongest, where he had elected to defend in depth and where, even if they were to break the French first line, the famed redcoats would still have to face the cream of the French cavalry, on level ground after having suffered several hours of continual bombardment by his artillery.

The Allied attempt to weaken his centre by attacking Fontenoy and the Antoing redoubts had been easily anticipated, but what had surprised him was the apparent decision by Cumberland not to vigorously contest the Bois de Barry. As he saw it, the managed woodland would provide his opponent with the opportunity to turn his left flank and roll up the French line from north to south. Saxe had no way of knowing that, not only had this manoeuvre been discussed at length during the enemy councils of war and vetoed by Cumberland, but also that its execution, albeit in a reduced and less adventurous form, was now being delayed by the indolence of a single British officer.

A short while later, as the Dutch fell back to lick their wounds, the Marquis de Beauffremont rode up to congratulate Saxe on his victory, but the old campaigner merely gestured eastwards, to where Ligonier's redcoats were

slowly forming up, saying, 'Look yonder. There are the British, and they will be a far more difficult meal to digest than what we have been served so far'.

Confident that this was indeed going to be the decisive engagement that he had sought, and that his opponent was committing his entire force to the battle, Saxe decided to remain cautious and leave Bérenger in position, instead sending a courier to Löwendahl ordering him to bring his forces southwards. He accepted that it would take the Dane some hours to marshal his troops and get them moving, but there was no longer any point in their being in position to thwart an enemy movement that would never come.

By 9.45am, Saxe could see the blue-coated Dutch infantry re-forming for another assault on Fontenoy, whilst a number of red-coated battalions were now moving from the enemy right in an obvious move to support the developing attack. Assured that Lutteaux was more than skilled enough to contain this latest enemy manoeuvre, and in order to ensure that the command of the Gardes Françaises remained in capable hands, Saxe instructed the Duc de Biron – commander of the Brigade du Roi – to assume overall direction of the Guards battalions in succession to the fallen Duc de Grammont, instructing him to withdraw his new command a short distance to the rear in order to bring them out of the line of sight of the British cannon which, having driven the French batteries back, were now plying their trade against the French infantry.

Commissioned by the Marquis d'Argenson, a close friend of Saxe, this painting by Pierre l'Enfant shows King Louis XV and the Dauphin observing as the French cavalry make a succession of charges against the British infantry, whilst fresh brigades are forming up, ready to be committed to action. Note that the king is dressed differently than in previous studies by l'Enfant. (Musée de l'Armée, Paris)

Even as one messenger rode off, another arrived, this one bearing a note to the effect that the Allies had massed a column of upwards of 8,000 men within the cover of the Bois de Barry, and that it was driving a wedge between the two redoubts manned by the Régiment d'Eu.

Abandoning his carriage, and sucking on a lead musket ball in order to assuage his wracking thirst, Saxe signalled to his groom to bring up his horse, mounting clumsily, his infirmity held in check by pure willpower. Assembling his aides and escort, he then rode towards the woods to evaluate the situation for himself, quickly snapping off a series of orders which would bring up the reserve infantry to counter the perceived threat. But before they had ridden far, a second rider spurred up and breathlessly advised the Marshal that the Allied column had left the trees and was assembling behind the main body. The column in question was, of course, the battalions of Ingoldsby's brigade repositioning themselves after abandoning the woods, which shows that neither of the combatant armies was immune to the vagaries of the 'fog of war'.

KÖNIGSEGG'S COUNSEL

Rallying his troops, Waldeck was now certain of two things. Firstly, that the enemy crossfire which had earlier mauled his command, had rendered untenable any further attempt to seize his original objectives, and secondly that with the troops he had under orders even the most realistic option open to him – an attack on Fontenoy itself – would be extremely difficult.

With a newly acquired sense of caution, he planned to abandon the divisional structure, instead concentrating together those battalions he felt would display the courage and cohesion needed to press home an attack whilst Cronström would rally and re-form those regiments that had been excluded from the operation with Hessen-Phillipsthal marshalling his cavalry to exploit the anticipated breakthrough. Additionally, an officer was sent to Cumberland advising him of the new plan to carry Fontenoy and asking for support from the right wing, again adding the rejoinder that without such reinforcement he would be unable to guarantee success.

With Ingoldsby's brigade now dissolved, Cumberland was already organizing the support that Waldeck had requested by transferring Colonel Scipio Duroure's regiment of foot and Sempill's highlanders under Sir Robert Munro – ordering them to engage the upper end of the village whilst the Dutch attacked around the churchyard and the southern end of the enemy works. If the two regiments could break into the French defences, they could easily be reinforced by the remainder of Ilten's troops, thus creating a secure flank when Ligonier attacked up the Chemin de Mons.

It was at this moment that Königsegg, previously the voice of caution in the Allied camp, chose to speak up again. Whilst a welcome reinforcement, the two British battalions would have no major effect on the outcome of Waldeck's planned attack. By his

Increasingly preferred as a personal weapon by infantry officers, this image shows the lock detail of one of the few surviving examples of a Dutch officer's fusil, which was recovered from the battlefield at Fontenoy. (Image reproduced with kind permission of the Musée d'Histoire militaire de la Ville de Tournai)

estimation there were now at least two full brigades of French infantry in Fontenoy, meaning that in order to carry them by storm, the Allies would need to commit a far stronger force than Waldeck was planning to commit.

Offering to co-ordinate the operation himself, and in addition to the deployment of Duroure's and Sempill's regiments, Königsegg requested the immediate assignment of Ilten's remaining troops and, perhaps most important of all, the battery of four British howitzers that stood silently on the roadway, waiting patiently for orders to advance. His plan was simple. Under cover of artillery fire, the Anglo-Hanoverians would attack the eastern face of the French defence works whilst Waldeck led his troops against the southern face and, with the village's defences engaged the whole of their length, the howitzers would switch targets, lobbing shells into the rear of the enemy positions to disrupt the movement of enemy reserves whilst the infantry overran the defences.

With full discretion to choose his men, Waldeck assembled several battalions in which he had the most faith, presumably the Gardes de Voet, Aylva, Constant-Rebecque, Salis and Stürler, forming them up in two compact lines, supported

Close-up image of Fontenoy Church showing the damage incurred during both the initial bombardment and the second Dutch attack on the village.

by half of the available light cannon which had – under Königsegg's recommendation – been concentrated into a number of ad hoc batteries, the other half being allocated to Cronström who was to take the remainder of the infantry and launch another spoiling attack on the enemy redoubts.

Having learned from bitter experience, it was clear to Waldeck that as both infantry groups closed with the enemy, their respective lines of advance would eventually create a gap between them. To counter this he placed Schlippenbach's brigade at the junction of the two divisions, with orders to prevent the French from exploiting this weakness and then, once the first cracks had begun to appear in the opposing lines, to charge into them at full speed and fall upon the enemy rear. At the other end of the Dutch line, Coenders was to gather all remaining mounted troops and screen it from enemy attack.

Shortly after 10.00am, the Allied artillery began its bombardment of Fontenoy and, after maybe 15–20 minutes of sustained fire, the Anglo-Hanoverian battalions began their advance. Aware that success rested on all elements striking the French line in a series of simultaneous hammer blows, Waldeck gave orders for his troops to move forward and, turning left, signalled for Cronström to move off and begin his approach, but nothing happened – the Dutch infantry remaining stationary as the French artillery above them began to spew fire in their direction. Galloping over to Cronström's command position, Waldeck remonstrated with his subordinate, telling him that the success of the whole attack now depended upon his infantry moving against their assigned objective. Exasperated and knowing that his presence was required with his own detachment, he relieved Cronström and transferred the command to Lt. Gen. von Schaumburg-Lippe, ordering him to comply with the existing orders.

Reluctantly, the blue-coated troops began to move forward, preceded by their light artillery, but, inevitably, as the French cannon opened fire, this part of the attack collapsed into a state of utter disorganization. Displaying

This painting of Fontenoy by William Skeoch Cumming, shows the Black Watch as they go prone in the face of enemy fire before launching their furious attack on the French defences. The commanding officer, Sir Robert Munro, famously remained standing during the enemy volley and remained unscathed by their fire. (Black Watch Museum, Balhousie Castle)

only marginally more élan than his commander, Schaumburg's advance was tortoise-like and the troops simply failed to press home, halting some distance from the French lines, their artillery deploying to engage the enemy positions with grapeshot.

Mindful of his orders, and possibly intent on alleviating Schaumburg's problems, Schlippenbach ordered his squadrons into the attack but, hit by musketry from several directions, the troopers lost all cohesion and scattered in disorder before falling back towards Bourgeon, where the Dutch brigadier rallied them as best he could. On the opposite end of the line, it was a similar story for – and as should have been anticipated – as soon as Coenders' cavalry began their own advance they were once again cruelly enfiladed by the French artillery before falling back in disorder towards the cover afforded by Péronnes.

Unaware of events behind him Waldeck pressed on but, as his men advanced into a storm of enemy fire, they were, like their comrades, stopped far short of their objective. Ignominiously they too soon fell back towards their start lines. Within four hours of their initial attack, the Army's left wing had collapsed and would play no further active role in the battle.

Whilst their comrades began their attack from the south, the six red-coated battalions aligned themselves so that they would come in on the flank of Waldeck's command, lapping around the defences, before rolling up the enemy line and splitting them in two. Having had the shortest distance to travel, the Hanoverian battalions of Oberg, Campe, Zastrow and Spörcken – under the command of Brigadier von Böselager – occupied the centre and left of the attack, whilst the two English regiments took the right under the overall direction of Colonel Duroure.

Having chafed under Ingoldsby's command, Munro led his Scotsmen enthusiastically forward and, as the words of command rang out from the village, he ordered them to go prone and allow the enemy fire to pass ineffectually over their heads before springing to their feet and continuing with their charge. A corpulent man, he himself stood with the regimental colours behind him, and when later – after the battle – he was praised for his valour in the face of the enemy, he remarked simply that had he followed his own orders he would have had the most extreme difficulty in standing up again.

At the French volley, the highlanders – as ordered – went prone and then, rising to their feet, charged the enemy positions. Pausing on the lip to deliver their own volley, the kilted warriors sprung down into the trench and, in a flurry of musket butts, bayonets and broadswords managed to capture a large section of the works – one highlander reportedly dispatching nine Frenchmen with nine strokes of his claymore before an enemy cannonball took off his arm. Munro's problem was that his men were now effectively in a ditch with the enemy's second line several feet above them, and there seemed no further way forward. A number of attempts were made to scale the earth rampart and clear a way through, but its height and a lack of success along the front as a whole meant that the highlanders could make no headway, and, with 136 of his men dead or wounded, Munro was forced to order a retreat, himself needing to be dragged bodily out of the enemy trench in order to avoid capture.

Alongside the highlanders, Duroure's companies had better going of it as, on the end of the French position, the defences were not as deep as those attacked by either Munro or the Hanoverians, a possible reason for this being that this was the area through which the supporting brigades would be committed, should the Allies attempt to carry the village.

Crashing into the ranks of the Beauvoisis regiment, the initial attack achieved significant local success, Duroure leading from the front, bravely brandishing a highland broadsword, but, as the redcoats drove forward trying to cut their way through to the highlanders, they were confronted by the arrival of a single battalion of the Régiment du Roi, which de Biron had earlier committed to the defence of the village, and which itself was now rushing into the combat to relieve the beleaguered Dauphin Brigade.

Looking north along the line of British advance to the ridgeline. The Gardes Françaises would have been initially deployed to the right of the road before being withdrawn in the face of the British artillery fire that led to the deaths of Grammont and Brocard.

The fighting now became desperate as growing numbers of Frenchmen entered the chaos of the mêlée, preventing the junction of the redcoats. At some stage during the combat, Duroure was badly wounded by a cannonball and carried to the rear, still clutching the hilt of his shattered claymore. As the vicious fighting continued, so rose the casualty list amongst the British officers – Lt. Col. Whitmore, Captain Campbell, Lieutenants Buckland and Lane, and Ensigns Cannon and Clifton were killed, whilst Major Cosseley, Captains Rainsford and Robinson, Lieutenants Townsend, Murray, Millington and Delgaire, and Ensigns Dagers and Pierce were all wounded to varying degrees, with a further three officers later reported missing, presumed captured. Of the rank and file, some five NCOs and 148 other ranks were killed during the street fighting, with almost the same number wounded. Pushed into an ever-decreasing perimeter, when the wounded Rainsford, by now the most senior officer still on his feet, grudgingly gave the order for the regiment to retire, less than half of its number emerged from the carnage unscathed.

Although the attacks on both their flanks would ultimately prove to be unsuccessful, it now fell to the Hanoverian Brigade to break into the enemy lines and salvage the situation, and the four battalions advanced at the double, determined to erase the continued slurs suffered at the hands of their British comrades, who still chided them for their perceived cowardice at Dettingen.

Like the highlanders, the German battalions slowly managed to fight their way into the French works, but in the face of the concentrated enemy fire they were unable to make real progress and, however unwilling, they eventually pulled back from the firing line rather than risk their possible destruction at the hands of the Dauphin Brigade, which by this stage had already thrown Waldeck's forces back in complete disarray and could now easily sweep down and wreck the brigade as a fighting force. Gradually and above all grudgingly, the red-coated troops disengaged from Fontenoy, harassing their opponents with long-range musketry as a way of maintaining a threat in being which would discourage them from depleting the garrison.

The fact that the French failed to grasp the opportunity to strike a death blow to the Allied plan is most likely down to two factors: firstly, the disarray caused by the Anglo-Hanoverian attack, and secondly the fact that when the defensive trace around Fontenoy was constructed, no provision had been made for the defenders to make a sally. But Lutteaux was not merely an aggressive commander he was an able one as well, and, fully appreciative of the threat still posed by the red-coated battalions, he knew that his first priority was to see to the needs of his troops. The fighting had been hard and, despite the ineffectual conduct of the Dutch, the Anglo-Hanoverians could quickly re-form for a fresh assault.

With the situation in Fontenoy stabilized, Lutteaux anticipated later events by sending orders to the officer commanding the Calonne bridgehead, instructing him forcibly to detain any troops caught trying to flee the battlefield and re-form them so that they could be returned

Looking north from behind the position of the Gardes Françaises. Infantry of the second line were deployed to the right, the cavalry to the left. Bérenger's corps was just over the horizon and Löwendahl's point of arrival near where the factory buildings stand today.

to the fighting. On his own initiative, Lt. Gen. Chabannes had performed a similar duty to the north of the Allied breakthrough, but although he was able to re-form a nominal number of units, they were very much weakened and of doubtful use in a counterattack against a formed and steady opponent.

Whilst contemporary French sources would later laud both the British and Hanoverian troops for the courage and bravery they displayed in charging into the maelstrom of fire that erupted around Fontenoy, little ink was spilt in a similar praise for the Dutch troops. For many, their regiments were no longer of the same martial calibre as those that had fought earlier in the armies of William III or the Duke of Marlborough, yet it must be acknowledged that even the bravest and best-led troops can falter in the face of a robust and well-planned defence, which is exactly what the Dutch came up against. It is unclear how well the Anglo-Hanoverians would have performed had they had to advance through the artillery crossfire that was to plague both Dutch attacks, and perhaps Louis XV was being rather ungracious when he laughingly instructed one of the battery commanders to have his men collect the spent Dutch cannonballs and fire them back at their original owners as he had no desire to remain in possession of such 'gifts'.

'MESSIEURS LES ANGLAIS, TIREZ LES PREMIERS!'

Towards 11.00am, Ligonier ordered Lewis to limber his pieces and bring them to the rear in order to clear the line of advance, sending word to Cumberland that his deployment was now complete and that he remained at the Duke's disposal for additional orders. It was once again one of those turning points during the battle in which the Allied Captain-General could have disengaged and cut his losses, electing to withdraw and engage Saxe in a war of manoeuvre, fully aware that the strength of his army could only increase as the campaigning season progressed, whilst that of the enemy could only decrease. However, deciding to risk all on the ability of the British infantry to break the enemy centre, and resolving to join the advance himself, Cumberland now gave Ligonier orders to prepare to attack.

The official report, written in the week following the battle would state: 'When our lines were drawn up in good order, with the cavalry behind them, H.R.H. put himself at their head and gave orders to march directly on the enemy. Prince Waldeck moved at the same time to attack Fontenoy, which the Left Wing did without effect [this was later rather diplomatically amended to 'faintly'], and during their march there was a most fearful fire of cannon.'

On one hand, it is clear that even at such a relatively short remove from the battle, excuses were being sought and rehearsed regarding why the Allied plan failed, but this quote shows that Cumberland had also taken into account the fact that, whilst the British remained uncommitted, the French could mass their reserves and attack the disorganized left wing, routing it and then placing the Anglo-Hanoverians in a position from which it would be difficult to escape. The

Looking east from the ridgeline to the position where the British delivered their initial volley, which had such a devastating effect on the French front line.

Duke had accepted the need for action, without any pretence of finesse, and, once joined by his commanding officer, Ligonier gave the signal to advance, the brigades of the first line stepping off, beginning the march that would take them up to the enemy and would write their names in the history books.

With drums beating and the regimental colours snapping in the wind, the red-coated battalions began their stately progress up the gentle slope towards the French brigades lining the gap between the village of Fontenoy and the Bois de Barry. Throughout the march, enemy round shot continued to strike the closed ranks, but thanks to Lewis's earlier action and the second attack on Fontenoy, the number of enemy cannon firing had by now been almost halved, the 'grand battery' described by some commentators comprising but eight guns at this time, four firing from the Redoute de Chambonas and possibly the same number being served from the Fontenoy defences.

Gradually the distance between the two lines reduced until only 80 paces separated the opposing forces, and it was now that one of the most iconic, analysed and disputed events of the battle took place.

As the red-coated line came to a halt, Captain Charles, the Lord Hay, of the 1st Foot Guards, left the British ranks and, advancing a few paces, doffed his tricorne and bowing to the enemy pulled a hip flask from his pocket, raising it in salute to the French guardsmen and taking a long drink

One of the iconic images of the battle, this painting by Félix Philippoteaux shows the moment when the British and French Guards salute each other before joining combat. A number of French casualties can be seen between the formations, showing how far the French had withdrawn to their new position. (Victoria & Albert Museum, London)

before – and by his own account – admonishing them for their previous conduct at Dettingen, enjoining them to stand and fight and not flee as they had done at the earlier battle. Turning, Hay then called upon his men to give three cheers for the enemy. Painfully aware of what Hay was offering, an unknown British soldier was reputedly heard to cry out, 'For what we are about to receive…'.

In response, Philippe, Comte d'Anterroches a grenadier lieutenant of the Gardes Françaises left his own unit and, like Hay, advanced into the space dividing the two lines of troops. Eagerly watched by his senior officers, the Frenchman offered his own reply to the British officer's salute and then began to harangue the enemy in his native language. Exactly what Anterroches said is unclear, but the version of events later recorded by the French writer Voltaire, has Hay offering to concede the advantage by suggesting that the French open fire first, the reason for this being that a unit's initial fire was often its most carefully loaded, and therefore its most effective. Not to be outdone, the French nobleman countered by refusing Hay's offer and chivalrously inviting the British themselves to fire the first volley.

One of the two protagonists of the meeting of the French and British Guards brigades – this uniform is a reconstruction of that worn by the Comte d'Anterroches as a Lieutenant de Grenadiers des Gardes Françaises. (Image copyright and reproduced with kind permission of Gabriele Mendella)

In any event, and before there could be any further exchange between the two officers, it was the defenders' fire discipline which failed first. From somewhere within the French ranks a random musket was discharged, then a second and a third until their entire line erupted in flame, albeit with minimal effect, and then having – as Ligonier laconically remarked 'received their fire' – the redcoats responded to the enemy volley. After the first 'firing' had discharged their muskets, the company officers suspended the firing cycle and, as they had done to such great effect at Dettingen, the British infantry doubled forward through the powder smoke until, at little more than 40 paces, they resumed the process, the discharges of the second and third firings slamming viciously into the French ranks at virtually point-blank range.

Under this concentrated fire, the French line first buckled and then recoiled in disarray as the British calmly reloaded, firing again into their already convulsed ranks. Although we have no real way in which to calculate exactly how deadly this initial volley was, the official final casualty lists for each of the four French regiments involved (Gardes Françaises – 411, Gardes Suisses – 226, Aubeterre – 328 and Courten – 301) give eloquent testament to the effect of the British fire discipline. From an approximate strength of 5,000 effectives almost one in four Frenchmen was either killed or wounded during the battle. It was, to paraphrase the author David Blackmore, both 'devastating and formidable'; indeed, it was later said of the Aubeterre regiment that its casualties were so numerous and had fallen in such perfect formation that its position in the French front line was instantly recognizable.

With the French trying to shore up the line with the redeployment of local reserves, and with circumstances changing on a minute-by-minute basis Cumberland was now forced to re-evaluate his whole battle plan. The Dutch under Waldeck had singularly failed in their objectives, but the Anglo-Hanoverian attack on Fontenoy had drawn at least one additional French brigade – Brigade du Roi – into the fighting and this formation would need time to reorganize before it could take further part in the battle. On the other

This aerial photograph of the village of Fontenoy shows the bottleneck through which the Allies hoped to force the 'Grand Column'. The blue elements represent the French positions, and the red, the advancing allies. The trace of the historical French defence works have been superimposed upon the modern buildings, whilst the modern sugar factory has been edited out and the Bois de Barry edited to reflect the historical tree line. In addition the two French redoubts have been added to show how they affected the Allied movement. (Image courtesy of Alain Bonnet, overlays by Séan O'Brogaín)

hand, failure had not been the exclusive preserve of the Dutch contingent and his attempt to secure the Bois de Barry and neutralize the Redoute de Chambonas had turned into a complete disaster. If he pressed on with the attack, he knew that this enemy bastion would pour fire into the flank of his advancing troops, and that many would pay with their lives before enough men could be brought forward from the rearmost brigades to mask it and take it by direct assault.

The situation facing the Duke was that with 18 battalions (the total would later increase to 21) – an estimated 16,000 men – he needed to push through the bottleneck between village and woodland, thereby gaining enough space for his troops to deploy and cover the advance of the Anglo-Hanoverian cavalry and artillery train. Naturally this had to be achieved whilst all the time beating off the inevitable enemy counterattacks, and it was a decision that Cumberland needed to make with only a partial overview of the enemy's deployment. On the other hand, the temptation was clearly there. His troops had just broken the Gardes Françaises and now seemingly all that stood between the Allies and a famous victory were but two lines of French cavalry. In addition to this, the ultimate prize – the capture of the French king and his heir – lay within his grasp. It was a decision at which many a more grizzled and experienced commander might have baulked but, caught up in the moment and without a single word of dissent from Ligonier riding at his side, Cumberland gave the order for the troops to continue their advance into the fields beyond Fontenoy.

Dressing ranks once more, the British infantry pressed on, the width of the gap and the threat from the remaining French cannon causing the lines instinctively to contract their frontage, and so now instead of two lines of infantry there were three or even four, the battalions deepening their formations so that the whole resembled what later commentators would describe as the 'grand column'.

To the rear, the Hanoverian – Zastrow – extemporized another infantry brigade by recalling Campe and Oberg's battalions from before Fontenoy, adding them to the two battalions (Pulteney's and Böselager's) that he had brought out of the Bois de Barry, and possibly drawing upon the battalion of Waldeck's regiment that had been assigned to Moltke's Reserve Corps.

Of Cumberland's initial plan to secure the woods, little remained, with the exception of the two Austrian *Freikorpskompagnien* maintaining a sporadic skirmish fire against the enemy to their front.

SAXE'S RIPOSTE

Although the almost contemptuous ease with which the British had swept aside the Gardes and Aubeterre brigades, the action itself and the potential crisis that it raised for Saxe's battle plan serves to underline the different command styles of the army commanders and why Saxe is remembered as one of history's great generals, whereas the Duke of Cumberland's conduct on 11 May 1745 is often used as grounds to view him as being more suited to command at a lower level.

Whilst Cumberland allowed himself to be 'drowned in the detail', as exemplified either by his handling of the Ingoldsby situation or indeed his actual joining of Ligonier's attack, his opponent remained more distant, preferring to review and prioritize developments, delegating where possible but maintaining his grip on the ebb and flow of battle.

Aware that a second Allied attack on Fontenoy had been thrown back with heavy loss, Saxe knew that the defending brigade and its supports would need time to re-form and resupply. Trusting that Lutteaux would be able to make the necessary dispositions, he relegated events around the village from the list of his immediate concerns.

Likewise, the Comte de Löwendahl, still en route to the battlefield, was not scheduled to arrive for some hours, which meant that he too had to be excluded from the French countermove and would likely arrive only either to exploit a French victory or to cover a French retreat.

View north-west from the Fontenoy defences across the site of the French camp to the cavalry deployment area. The foreground would have been occupied by the Régiment du Roi, which was deployed to provide immediate support should the village be attacked and also to provide cover should it be outflanked by an Allied attack.

The most junior element of the Maison du Roi were the Grénadiers à Cheval, who were organized into a single company of 90 men, and whose captain was the King of France himself. This reconstruction is of the uniform of a grenadier as he would have appeared in 1745. (Image copyright and reproduced with kind permission of Gabriele Mendella)

The only priority with which Saxe had to concern himself at this moment was therefore to plug the gap, stabilize the front line and then to repulse the enemy attack. As a result he sent word to Bérenger, apprising him of the situation and instructing him to reposition his forces in order to release at least a brigade of foot for immediate transfer to the right flank. He then took time to send a courier to the royal party suggesting that, on account of the proximity of the enemy and for safety reasons, the king's headquarters be moved farther to the rear.

On the firing line, officers still continued trying to instil some form of cohesion within the ranks of the shattered battalions, and with the Brigade du Roi committed to the defence of Fontenoy, Saxe rode up to the commander of the Royal Vaisseaux, ordering him to take his troops forward. This local reinforcement was a stopgap measure, aimed at reducing the disparity in numbers, and as a next step an officer was sent to the Comte de Thomond, in command of the Irish Brigade, ordering him to wheel his battalions to their right from their position from behind the Bois de Barry, and to prepare to take the advancing British in their open flank.

But the Irishmen would need some time to change formation and adequately prepare for the attack and, with the enemy about to resume their bloody advance, time was the one thing that Saxe had little of. Playing the last card that he had at his immediate disposal, he ordered the first line of French cavalry to advance into contact. At best, they would halt the enemy and throw them back, at worst they would buy enough time for Saxe to co-ordinate his infantry counterattack adequately.

THE BOTTLENECK

The disorganized foe to their front, the British infantry – now six battalions abreast – continued steadily forward, advancing into the artillery crossfire. Undeterred by the deadly hail, the redcoats pressed stoically onward and, as a halt was made to dress ranks, the hoarse cries of the officers could be heard calling for the supporting artillery to be dragged forward and manhandled into position.

Ahead of the British, a dull thudding of hooves could be heard, and with cries of 'Ware cavalry' the line refused its flanks, officers urging their men into formation, the battalion intervals now studded with the 3lb cannon so laboriously dragged forward by the grenadier companies. Sweeping into view came four regiments of French cavalry (Royal Cravattes, Fiennes, Clermont-Prince and FitzJames) – almost 2,500 men – under the Comte d'Estrées, their numbers augmented by noble officers from other regiments who had simply abandoned their posts, determined to be amongst those who struck the first blow for France.

As the mass of man and horseflesh thundered towards the stationary British line, officers sought to calm their men as the crisp and precise words of command rose from the ranks. As one, a steady row of muskets was raised and hammers cocked, bayonets glittering as they pointed defiantly at the

French cavaliers. Then as the horsemen were about 50 yards (46m) distant the orders rang out and thousands of muskets belched flame, their staccato report punctuated by artillery fire. This physical blow halted the horsemen who, despite a small number that had been unable to stop their horses from crashing uncontrolledly into the waiting enemy, now milled in front of them, firing pistols, unable to close and engage the British in hand-to-hand combat.

Estrées had done exactly what had been asked of him and had stopped the British advance dead in its tracks, gaining precious time for Saxe to continue his preparations for a counterstroke, but in doing so his own troops had forgone the mobility that made them the 'Queen of the Battlefield' and they now stood blown and disordered in front of a formed British line quickly reloading its weapons. To stand and continue would have sacrificed the cavalry to no real purpose and so the only sensible course of action was to withdraw towards the Bois de Barry and the shelter of the infantry assembling there so that, in doing so, he uncovered the brigades of Couronne and Royal which Saxe had marshalled into position moments before.

It was by now some time after midday and, as the French cavalry disengaged, Ligonier gave the command for the infantry to advance once more, fully prepared to deal with the enemy line infantry as he had their guards. But with every minute that passed, with every step that was taken, the tactical situation changed. Ligonier would later state that, in his estimation, at this time the British column had progressed almost 300 paces from where it had brushed the French guards aside, whereas French accounts tend to suggest that the distance covered was only half that. In any event, this was no longer a battle of manoeuvre but rather one of endurance, the main – and perhaps only – question being whether or not the British formation would collapse before it had exhausted the ability of its opponents to fight.

View northward from the Fontenoy defences across the deployment area of the French reserve infantry. It was here that Saxe would assemble the southern prong of his attack on the Anglo-Hanoverians. With the northern prong unable to advance, it was thrown back with the loss of the Marquis de Lutteaux, but blocked Cumberland's attempt to change the direction of his advance and outflank the Fontenoy defences.

With the confusion of close combat magnified by the clouds of musket smoke which hung over the British infantry, this painting by Charles Parrocel – *The Cavalry Attack* – gives a good impression of the chaos and carnage as the French cavalry repeatedly charged the British ranks in an attempt to slow the Allied advance and give Saxe the time he badly needed to rally his disorganized forces and prepare his counterstroke.

FRENCH

1. Piémont
2. Crillon
3. Bettens
4. Dragoons (Dismounted)
5. Dauphin
6. Roi
7. Aubeterre
8. Gardes Françaises
9. Gardes Suisses
10. Royal
11. Couronne
12. Royal Vaisseaux
13. Irlandais
14. Eu
15. Arquebusiers de Grassin
16. Colonel-Général
17. Clermont-Prince
18. Royal Cravattes
19. Royal Rousillon
20. Royal Étranger
21. Brionne
22. Noailles
23. Gendarmerie
24. Maison du Roi

SAXE ××××

EU ×××

LUTTEAUX ×××

ANTOING

FONTENOY

▼ EVENTS

1. The Allied right wing forms up in two lines west of Vezon, each of three infantry brigades. Under fire from the French cannon on the ridgeline above, Ligonier asks for artillery support to suppress the enemy guns. British field train under Col. Lewis engages French field artillery with counterbattery fire, destroying a number of guns and forcing the remainder that are deployed in the open to be withdrawn, the only batteries remaining in operation are those in Fontenoy and the Redoute de Chambonas. During this phase both the Duc de Grammont and the Marquis de Brocard are killed.

2. Forced to contract its frontage on account of the bottleneck, the Allied right wing, now resembling what is later referred to as 'the grand column', advances to its second position and, following the incident between Lord Hay and the Comte d'Anterroches, engages the enemy in a firefight. The French fire is largely ineffective, but with two close-range volleys the Allies shatter the leading French brigades, effectively breaking the infantry line by forcing it to recoil.

3. The Allied infantry now reach their third position and begin to adopt an open square formation. The Guards Brigade occupies the right or northern face, the Royals the centre or western face and Onslow's the left or southern face. As the column advances, the left and right faces are expanded by Sowle's and Howard's brigades respectively, with Zastrow's ad hoc brigade operating as a tactical reserve. The opportunity is now taken to bring the supporting light artillery forward and to integrate the cannon into the front line.

4. In an effort to check the Allied advance, and in order to gain time for their foot to reorganize, the French first-line cavalry make a succession of charges against the square. The attacks are successfully beaten off with loss but succeed in so far as the forward momentum of the grand column is severely reduced, ultimately coming to a halt some 200–300 yards (170–280m) from the point where the French front line was broken. With mounting losses and a lack of cohesion the Allies need to stand and re-form if any further progress is to be made.

5. Unable to push through the area occupied by the square, the Allied cavalry remains stationary awaiting developments and further orders.

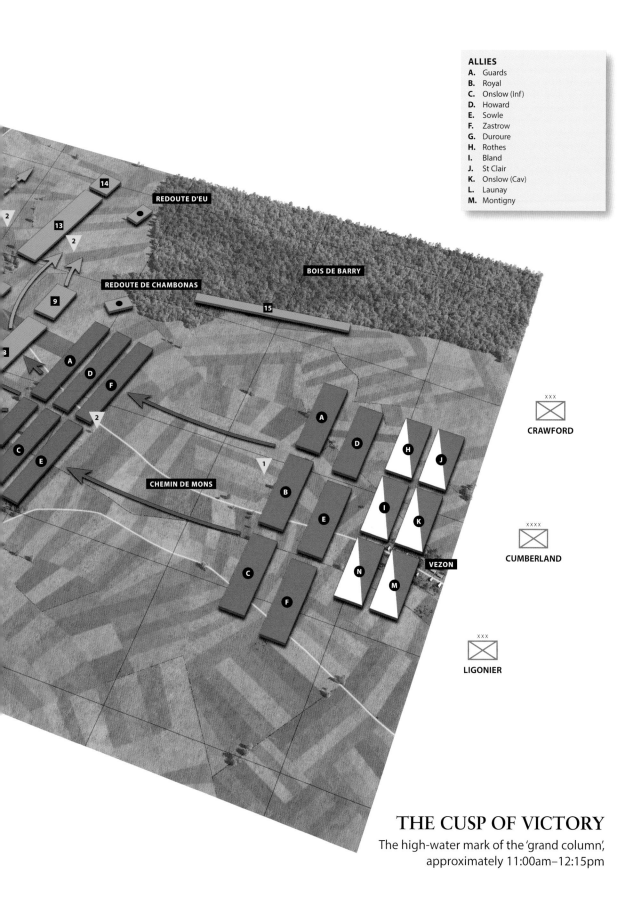

ALLIES
A. Guards
B. Royal
C. Onslow (Inf)
D. Howard
E. Sowle
F. Zastrow
G. Duroure
H. Rothes
I. Bland
J. St Clair
K. Onslow (Cav)
L. Launay
M. Montigny

REDOUTE D'EU

BOIS DE BARRY

REDOUTE DE CHAMBONAS

CHEMIN DE MONS

VEZON

CRAWFORD

CUMBERLAND

LIGONIER

THE CUSP OF VICTORY
The high-water mark of the 'grand column',
approximately 11:00am–12:15pm

Although it looked to many as if the redcoats were unstoppable, Saxe continued with his task, frantically directing his troops to new positions, garnering his strength and slowly a new line began to take shape. Anchoring on the Redoute de Chambonas, Thomond placed his first three battalions (Berwick, Lally, Rooth) in position, ready to charge into the British right flank, with the Royal Vaisseaux under the Comte de Guerchy, falling into line as a second rank, their eight cannon providing a welcome reinforcement to Soubise's tiring gunners.

Directly to their right, the horsemen of the Royal Rousillon Brigade, deploying deeper than regulations dictated, formed a hinge between Thomond and the Couronne and Royal brigades, their own left flank covered by the cavalry of Brancas and Colonel-Général under the command of the Duc d'Harcourt, a living cul-de-sac into which the British had to advance if they wished to hold the field.

Satisfied that he had stabilized the situation, Saxe now felt able to report to the king, and on reaching the royal headquarters he found it in an uproar, with rival groups each trying to persuade King Louis XV to follow its suggested course of action. At the head of one group stood Noailles, convinced that the progress of the seemingly unstoppable British column presaged a catastrophic French defeat and that the king should quit the field, whilst leading the others was the Duc de Richelieu, nephew of the great Cardinal and certainly no friend to Saxe, who repeatedly warned his royal master that flight would itself be the catalyst for defeat.

Dismounting painfully, Saxe reached the king, bowed and turning to the assembled nobles growled – in language more suited to the backstreets of either Paris or Dresden – that no man of honour would leave the field before the battle was declared lost. It is a moment in the course of the battle that is literally open to interpretation, and a modern biography of Saxe reports his words as being simply, 'Which of you _ _ _ _ gave His Majesty that piece of advice?'

Leading the king forward, he took a proffered telescope, and brought the advancing red juggernaut into focus for his sovereign. Next he picked out the infantry of Couronne and Royal standing resolutely in the enemy's path, flanked by Harcourt's remaining cavalry, and explained to the king their current orders. Scanning farther right he described the edge of the Bois de Barry where the cannon still thundered and the ranks of infantry waited impatiently for the order to attack, and the remnants of the Gardes, its members battered and apprehensive but assuredly ready to do their duty. Sweeping the glass farther north he picked out a further brigade of infantry – Normandie – moving southwards in response to his earlier message to Bérenger. And then, finally, the king's vision rested upon the proud horsemen of the Maison du Roi and the Carabiniers. Aware that not just the outcome of this battle but perhaps of the entire campaign rested upon the answer to his next question, Saxe took a deep breath and calmly asked Louis for permission to commit the elite cavalry.

THE 'GRAND COLUMN'

Advancing steadily, the Allied column's strength was its own primary weakness for the farther it moved into the enemy lines, the more troops had to be diverted to cover its extending flanks, and so from initially being a close-packed mass of infantry lines, it soon became what would later be referred to as a hollow square, open towards its rear. Six battalions faced north towards the thickening French lines near the Bois de Barry, three battalions westwards towards Couronne and Royal, whilst a further eight covered the approaches to Fontenoy, with Zastrow holding four battalions in reserve in the middle – Böselager and Oberg at the front, Pulteney and Campe to the rear. Within the whole, detachments of men scurried about, busily gathering ammunition from the dead and dying whilst members of the artillery train used the slow progress as an opportunity to repair damaged cannon or to bring into action any serviceable French pieces that had been overrun.

It was about 12.30pm and, confident that the time was ripe, Saxe quickly drafted a plan in which the now-rallied Aubeterre Brigade, together with Couronne and Royal would overwhelm the western face of the Allied square, whilst Thomond and Guerchy – supported by the Normandie Brigade – would crash into the northern side of the enemy formation, cutting it in two. It would be 22, predominantly fresh, French battalions facing half their number of Anglo-Hanoverians, an enemy that had been the target of an intense cannonade for some hours.

It should have been a forgone conclusion, but for an illustration of what Saxe believed to be one of the fundamental faults of the French military: a more than ever present likelihood that a senior officer would disobey orders on a whim without thought for the consequences, secure in the knowledge that he would not be punished for his actions.

In the wake of Estrées's withdrawal, and Saxe's impromptu strategy meeting with the king, the Comte d'Apcher, seeking to garner fame as the man who broke the Allies, launched an ill-considered attack with the cavalry under his command, the two regiment-brigades of Brionne and Noailles and the single regiment of Berry. Thundering towards the western and north-western faces of the square, the mass of the French cavalry were halted by a well-aimed volley from the redcoats, but the men of Noailles cut their way into the ranks of the 3rd Foot Guards and out of the other side before crashing into the battalions of the reserve. Of their leading squadron, only 14 men survived – ten of these as prisoners, their colours falling into Hanoverian hands.

Compounding the error, Estrées now ordered the cavalry of the Royal Roussillon Brigade forward in an attempt to cover Apcher's retreat, but served only to create a confusing situation whereby the cavalry's flight – aided by British musketry – prevented the advance of the Irish Brigade, meaning that Saxe's counterstroke would go in at only less than half of its planned strength.

Conferring with Ligonier, and sensing the hesitation in the enemy ranks, Cumberland instructed the Earl of Albemarle to order the 2nd Guards to break ranks and double towards the nearest enemy to give them a close-range volley. The resulting fire threw the Royal Vaisseaux into disorder and Cumberland used this development to his advantage, changing the angle of the Allied advance so that the redcoats veered away from the Bois de Barry, inclining instead towards the northern end of Fontenoy itself. His aim was

Ranking third in the regiments comprising the Maison du Roi, the Chevaulégers de la Garde du Roi, was composed of a single company of eight officers and 220 *maîtres* and entry was restricted to officers of noble birth. Virtually annihilated at Dettingen in 1742, the unit was reconstituted and saw extensive service in 1745. In the field, King Louis XV habitually wore the uniform of regimental captain. (Image copyright and reproduced with kind permission of Gabriele Mendella)

now to capture the end of the village, thereby freeing up the battalions still keeping the Dauphin Brigade in check, and by doing so open the Chemin de Mons not only for the redeployment of the artillery train – which would then be able to enfilade any French troops moving south from the tree line – but also for the eventual introduction of the Anglo-Hanoverian cavalry into the battle.

Even had he wanted to, there was simply no opportunity for Saxe to rescind or amend his orders for the attack. He had to trust that the three brigades – of which two were admittedly fresh – would obey orders and successfully press home the attack. Placing himself at the head of the Régiment Royal, and seeing that the British advance was being hampered by the need to maintain formation whilst the troops climbed over the piles of French dead which lay to their front, Lutteaux whirled his sword around his head and, levelling it at the enemy ranks, gave the order to charge.

Once more rank upon rank of British muskets belched flame and, as the attacking battalions staggered under the impact of the hail of bullets, Lutteaux fell fatally wounded at the head of his men. Crashing into each other, the two lines pirouetted in the deadly ballet of clubbed muskets and flashing bayonets, but the Frenchmen found no way through the enemy and, taking heavy losses, they withdrew south-west, not knowing that even in this local defeat they had more than kept Saxe's battle plan alive; in doing so they had effectively closed the gap through which Cumberland had hoped to outflank the Fontenoy defences and regain the initiative.

THE BALANCE SWINGS

As Lutteaux made his attack, King Louis ordered the Comte de Montesson, to advance the Maison du Roi and Carabiniers and form a rallying point for their shaken comrades, but no sooner had the flower of the French cavalry taken up position, than they launched themselves forward without orders in an attempt to break the Allied ranks with a combination of zeal and martial fervour.

Thundering towards the enemy, the elite horsemen were unable to press home their attack, many saddles being emptied by the devastating enemy musketry, before they were forced to drag their mounts bodily round and gallop away from a seemingly unbeatable foe.

With the notable exception of Saxe himself who refused to believe in anything other than a French victory, a sense of pessimism now began to pervade the French high command. Ever since the British had become engaged, it seemed as if there was nothing that could be done to stop them – firstly the Garde Françaises had been contemptuously swept aside, then the French cavalry had wrecked themselves in a series of fruitless charges against the red-coated ranks, next Lutteaux's charge had failed and now the elite of the army had also broken itself upon the British bayonets. It seemed to many that there was no available tactic, no card to play that would hurl the column back in disorder.

Once again Noailles gave voice to his opinion that the royal party should cross the Scheldt to safety, but this time King Louis refused even to countenance such a suggestion. He had placed his trust in a commander who had served France ably for years and he would not revoke that trust.

Fighting off the exhaustion that was threatening to incapacitate him and force him to hand the command of the army to a subordinate who would undoubtedly order the retreat, Saxe was convinced that the British superiority was an illusion that could and would still be shattered. The local attacks that he had ordered – and admittedly those that he had not ordered – had achieved their primary objective in that the enemy column had not merely been slowed but had been halted. In addition to this, he remained convinced that the key to victory lay in Cumberland's failure to seize either Fontenoy or the Redoute de Chambonas. He naturally had no way of knowing at this time that Cumberland had actually intended to force an entry into Fontenoy, or that the planned attack had been inadvertently thwarted by the withdrawal of Lutteaux's brigades.

The high-water mark. The area over which the British column made its farthest advance. Accounts disagree about exactly how far the Allies progressed before the advance slowed, but it is certain that they at least reached the line of barbed wire where the ploughed land gives way to the grassy fields.

The new plan that was developing in his mind was to concentrate as much artillery as possible against the Anglo-Hanoverians whilst again massing fresh brigades for a decisive attack. The Irish Brigade had still to see action, whilst the three battalions of Royal Vaisseaux were still relatively intact and the fresh Normandie was coming up to the front line, bringing the number of battalions up to 13. In addition to these, Löwendahl was approaching at the head of the Touraine and Auvergne brigades, which would add a further seven battalions to the total at his disposal. The Dane would also be bringing two fresh cavalry brigades, one of which was the Cuirassiers, and these would be welcome reinforcement should the enemy cavalry ever get into action.

It was approaching 1.00pm and it was clear to both commanders that the battle would be decided by the fighting on the Allied right wing. Ever since the failure of his second attack on Fontenoy, Waldeck, had been unable to marshal his troops for another attack, the men simply being unwilling to run the gauntlet of artillery fire that they knew awaited them. Instead, they relegated themselves to the role of mere spectators, their reluctance serving to give the enemy the option of redeploying a number of units to meet the Anglo-Hanoverian threat.

Again, the most precious commodity available to Saxe was time. If the Allies were to mount a determined attack, the chances were that it would be successful, and so he needed to give an illusion of strength which would give Cumberland pause for thought. With its left flank firmly anchored on the village of Fontenoy, the French front line now described an arc, drawn across the Allies' anticipated line of advance. Within the village, the Dauphin Brigade stood firm, its men bloodied but now in no real danger from a Dutch attack, and then extending the line farther to their left came the brigades du Roi, Aubeterre, Couronne and Royal – 16 battalions strong – supported by the French second-line cavalry, which had yet to see action. On Royal's own left flank massed the first-line cavalry, the Maison du Roi and then the Carabiniers. Despite being disorganized by the earlier fighting, this was still a potent force, its presence acting as an obvious deterrent to the Anglo-Hanoverians from making an all-out attack to break the French brigades to their front. Such a manoeuvre would obviously be complicated by the abundance of enemy

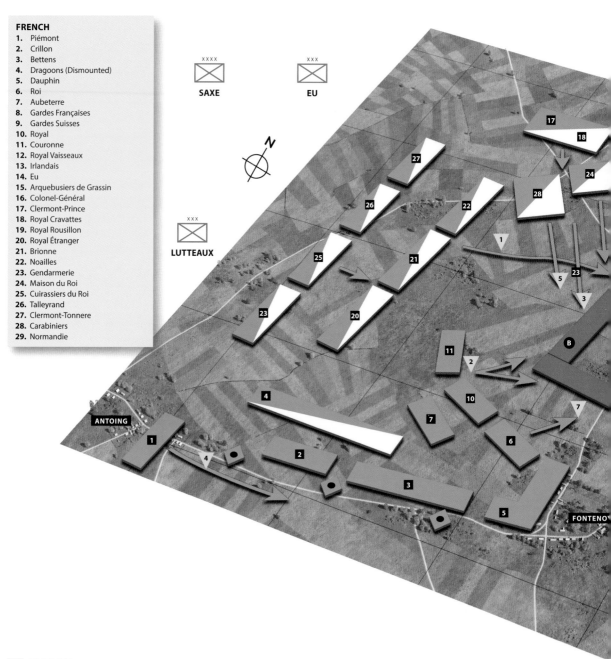

FRENCH

1. Piémont
2. Crillon
3. Bettens
4. Dragoons (Dismounted)
5. Dauphin
6. Roi
7. Aubeterre
8. Gardes Françaises
9. Gardes Suisses
10. Royal
11. Couronne
12. Royal Vaisseaux
13. Irlandais
14. Eu
15. Arquebusiers de Grassin
16. Colonel-Général
17. Clermont-Prince
18. Royal Cravattes
19. Royal Rousillon
20. Royal Étranger
21. Brionne
22. Noailles
23. Gendarmerie
24. Maison du Roi
25. Cuirassiers du Roi
26. Talleyrand
27. Clermont-Tonnere
28. Carabiniers
29. Normandie

SAXE

EU

LUTTEAUX

ANTOING

FONTENO

▼ EVENTS

1. Without orders, the Comte d'Apcher leads the Brionne and Noailles cavalry brigades into an attack of the Allied square. Although the attack is stopped by British fire, the lead squadron of Noailles breaks into the Allied formation where it is decimated. The Rousillon Brigade is thrown forward to cover d'Apcher's withdrawal and prevents the Irish Brigade from launching an attack on the British Guards.

2. Cumberland seizes the initiative by ordering a spoiling attack on the Royal Vaisseaux aimed at allowing him to realign the axis of the Allied attack towards Fontenoy. Lutteaux leads the Royal, Couronne and Aubeterre brigades against the southern face of the Allied square and is mortally wounded at the head of the Régiment Royal. The French are forced back, but effectively block the Allies' line of advance.

3. The Maison du Roi and Carabiniers advance to screen the re-forming French cavalry, and maintain pressure on the Allied square. No sooner are they in position than they attack without orders and are easily beaten off by the leading British battalions.

4. The Brigade de Piémont is ordered out of Antoing to put pressure upon the Dutch and prevent them from taking further part in the fighting.

5. Supported by a 4lb battery, and followed by the mass of the French cavalry, the Maison du Roi and the Carabiniers launch an attack against the western face of the Allied square. Simultaneously the Irish Brigade and Royal Vaisseaux make their attack against the British Guards, but are stalled until Normandie advances onto the disordered enemy flank.

6. Under attack from all sides except the rear, the Allied formation begins to buckle but does not break. After consultation with his senior commanders, Cumberland gives the order to withdraw, and the Allied right wing begins to conduct a fighting retreat towards Vezon. As it does so, Duroure's ad hoc brigade follows suit and Crawford orders the Allied cavalry forward to cover the retrograde movement.

7. Saxe now orders a general advance but the French now face the same problems as the British had done at the beginning of the battle and are unable to bring their superior numbers to bear, allowing the Allies to disengage, withdrawing through Vezon en route to Ath. Cumberland sends a courier to Waldeck informing him of his plans and the Dutch likewise withdraw.

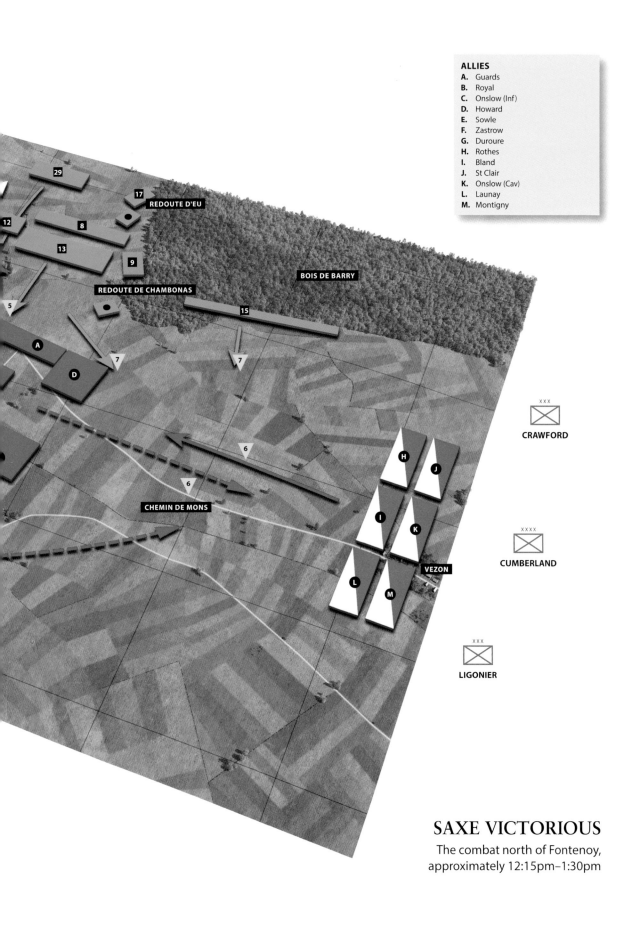

ALLIES
A. Guards
B. Royal
C. Onslow (Inf)
D. Howard
E. Sowle
F. Zastrow
G. Duroure
H. Rothes
I. Bland
J. St Clair
K. Onslow (Cav)
L. Launay
M. Montigny

REDOUTE D'EU

REDOUTE DE CHAMBONAS

BOIS DE BARRY

CHEMIN DE MONS

VEZON

CRAWFORD

CUMBERLAND

LIGONIER

SAXE VICTORIOUS
The combat north of Fontenoy,
approximately 12:15pm–1:30pm

horsemen and, although the redcoats had already beaten off several charges by pure firepower, it would still require adequate planning, sufficient ammunition and above all co-ordination between the units to ensure that the attack would run smoothly. If the line buckled or fractured, it would spell disaster and the right wing of the Pragmatic Army would simply disintegrate.

Events were now moving quickly and, as Normandie arrived to take its place in the line, it meant that Saxe had some 35 battalions facing the Allied column, which was by now, to all intents and purposes, a hollow square. On paper at least, this was a significant advantage, but the French marshal knew many of his troops had already suffered under the British volley fire, and it would be difficult to get them to advance into such an inferno again.

Having already intervened once to Saxe's benefit, Richelieu did so once more. Having seen an artillery battery, seemingly without orders, he immediately sent an aide to their commander with orders to bring them up to the front line. Carefully siting them opposite the right-hand corner of the British position, Richelieu made sure that they could enfilade any advance that the enemy would choose to make. Certain that this would be the point of decision, it was here that Saxe chose to make his final command post, and here that he turned to see Löwendahl who, at the head of the Brigade de Cuirassiers, had ridden ahead to gain a better understanding of the tactical situation on the battlefield. Embracing his friend and colleague, Saxe swept an arm in the direction of the enemy saying, 'This will be a fine day for his Majesty – Those people there, they cannot beat us now'.

THE FRENCH ATTACK

That Saxe could still function as a commander at this time of the day was nothing other than exceptional – despite his illness he had been in the saddle for several hours, working at a pace that would have exhausted a lesser man, but, having lost Lutteaux in the earlier combat, he now turned to Löwendahl – his most trusted subordinate – giving him command of the infantry intended to attack the northern face of the enemy formation.

In the centre of the field, the situation was becoming a bloodbath with the British volleys thundering out, crashing relentlessly into the ranks of French troops who were standing a scant 100 yards (92m) away, with the French returning fire from several artillery batteries, the round shot lancing through the red-clad lines from all points of the compass save the rear.

His preparations complete, Löwendahl rode to the Marquis de Créqui, at the head of the Carabiniers, telling him that the signal to charge would be when 'Richelieu's' battery had finished firing several salvoes at the column's right flank. Accordingly, the horsemen stoically received the enemy's fire, and then, as the final discharge echoed across the field, they spurred their mounts forward. In the words of one of their officers:

It was a horrible, terrible time and needed to be resolved quickly. To that end we had been deployed alongside the Maison, who were but 200 paces from the enemy, and we even closer. For a good quarter of an hour we stood there, without further orders and during this time we lost heavily through the enemy musketry and the grapeshot of their cannon… Then, as the infantry to our left moved into position, the order came for the Carabiniers to charge the enemy, but the attack never developed as planned and we were, it must be admitted, thrown back in chaos and disorder.

But uncertainty was visible on both sides, as Königsegg himself who had – uniquely – seen the action on both wings at first hand wrote: 'Following the failed attack by our Left Wing, the enemy threw his strength against the British who had already taken severe losses. Eventually they could no longer endure this heavy fire and their lines began to waver; but the Duke of Cumberland, through his courage and presence of mind rallied them and led them once more against the foe'.

Amongst the red-coated ranks, Cumberland, Königsegg, Ligonier and Albemarle were everywhere, cajoling their troops, exhorting them to one last effort, one last push that would sweep the enemy from the field and crown the Army with a victory as glorious as Dettingen had been. But the enemy fire had taken its toll and losses were mounting with many senior and regimental officers now casualties; Robert Carpenter and Henry Ponsonby had both been killed at the head of their brigades, whilst the badly wounded Charles Howard refused to be taken from the battlefield.

The failure either to neutralize the Rédoute de Chambonas or to turn the Fontenoy defences now came back to haunt Cumberland, the bitter truth being that – with the build-up of French troops to the north – his men were 'caught between a rock and a hard place', and in a hurried conference with his senior officers it was agreed that, without the likelihood of any tangible support from the Dutch, the position was no longer tenable and the right wing would need to withdraw out of the deadly crossfire and reconsider its options. It was a decision that was not taken lightly, but neither was it taken in a spirit of despair or futility. The question was how best to effect a withdrawal when the enemy was tangibly superior in all arms.

For the pugnacious Cumberland, the answer was simple: another limited counterattack, under cover of which the remainder of the troops would pull back a short distance and re-form, with the attacking troops retiring through them. When all was ready, the order was given and once again the British advanced against the foe and gave them a close-range volley. It was not truly effective, but it was sufficient to throw the enemy back in confusion and for a few moments it seemed as if Cumberland had in fact pulled something out of the hat as French troops fleeing past Louis XV and the Dauphin once more raised cries for the royal party to be evacuated to safety.

The moment of victory was a fleeting one, and as the British began their staggered withdrawal, the French launched their attack: from the west, the brigades du Roi, la Couronne

Excavation of common grave on the battlefield from which the bodies of 12 British soldiers were exhumed. (Image reproduced with courtesy and kind permission Alain Tripnaux)

'PLUGGING THE GAP' – THE RIDGELINE, APPROXIMATELY 12.45PM, TUESDAY 11 MAY 1745 (PP. 80–81)

With the French infantry shattered by British volleys, and needing to buy time and slow down the enemy advance, Saxe had only one card to play and that was to throw his cavalry brigades at the Anglo-Hanoverian column. If the troopers could break into the enemy formation it would be all well and good, but the priority was to delay the redcoats and prevent them from exploiting what was seemingly an inevitable victory.

After several unsuccessful charges had been made against the Anglo-Hanoverian column, and the battered cavalrymen withdrawn, it was now the turn of the Régiment Royal de Carabiniers **(1)**, the elite of the line cavalry, to take their turn in the attack. The Carabiniers were truly an elite unit, re-formed by Louis XIV in 1690, at Fontenoy; they comprised ten squadrons organized into five brigades and mounted on coal black horses, the rank and file carrying a rifled carbine and bayonet. Unlike other regiments in the Army, commissions were made by royal appointment and promotions by merit, which meant that the Carabiniers stood outside the normal purchase system.

Believing that the British line was on the point of collapse the French cavaliers charged *en fourage*, a slightly open order,

intending to force a breach in red-coated ranks with pistol fire. Coming up against the Royal Scots **(2)**, the senior line infantry regiment of the British Army, the result was a one-sided affair with the Frenchmen being forced to retire and re-form.

Aware that they need to maintain their cohesion or face disaster, the officers of the Royal Scots **(3)** push men back into line, ensuring that no gaps open in the line, that the enemy is always presented a threatening rank of bayoneted muskets.

To the right of the Royal Scots, the corner of the open square is occupied by the men of the 2nd Foot Guards **(4)**, who are now coming under attack from French troops moving south from the Bois de Barry **(5)**. It is at this point that the French cavalry will indeed break into the Allied formation, but the success will be short lived with the entire 1st squadron of the Régiment de Noailles either becoming casualties or being taken prisoner.

Eventually the sheer weight of French cavalry will force the Anglo-Hanoverians to halt and then, as fresh infantry are committed, they are forced to conduct a fighting retreat towards their starting positions around Vezon.

and Royal began their advance against the British left flank, whilst, sword drawn, Löwendahl ordered the Irish Brigade forward in the charge that would become synonymous with the battle, with both the Gardes Françaises and Normandie advancing in close support, they crashed into the British Guards.

Tradition has it that as the Irishmen moved into the attack a cry rose up from their ranks: '*Cuimhnígí ar Luimneach agus ar fheall na Sasanach!*' which translates as 'Remember Limerick and the Saxon perfidy', a reference to the Treaty of 1691, regarded by many as having been broken by King William III before the ink was dry on the document. Opinion is divided about whether the cry was uttered at all or indeed after half a century in French service, how much of the brigade actually had a fluent command of the Gaelic language. What is more than likely is one of the senior brigade officers shouted the words before giving the order to advance, and that in the intervening years one man's cry has been magnified into a thousand voices.

The ensuing combat soon became a scrum at bayonet point, with neither side conceding ground, and, although Sergeant Wheelock of Bulkeley's regiment is credited with capturing a colour of the 2nd Foot Guards, the mêlée remained a stalemate until the advent of Normandie on the Irish right flank.

Charging some enemy cannon at the point of the bayonet, the Frenchmen relieved the pressure on their compatriots and then – slowly – one step at a time began to push the British back. In the words of one of the French lieutenants:

> We advanced, and came across three of our Irish battalions who were being badly handled by the enemy, but our approach fortified them and they renewed the attack. To our front stood six enemy cannon and we had no choice but to charge them head on, even as they fired upon us at close range. In less than four minutes the enemy grapeshot had killed or wounded 16 officers and 250 men. This failed to stop us and as we overran the guns we forced the enemy to retire.

With the Anglo-Hanoverians starting to recoil, Saxe now unleashed his cavalry once more and – led by the Carabiniers and the Maison – the French cavaliers crashed into the disordered ranks, driving them back, and also creating chaos within the ranks of the Irish Brigade whose red coats were easily mistaken for those of the enemy. Having suffered the Allied fire for so long, and with their opponents falling back before them, the French cavalry, especially the Carabiniers, seemingly lost their heads and with cries of 'Onwards comrades – Destroy them!' plunged into the retreating battalions.

Looking westwards from the site of the mass grave towards Fontenoy defences, the clump of trees to the left marks the position of the Régiment de Beauvoisis. The line of trees to the far right marks the Antoing–Fontenoy defensive positions, which were attacked by the Dutch.

Sources differ about the immediate character of the Allied withdrawal. French sources would seem to indicate a precipitate flight, whilst British accounts convey the image of a staged withdrawal. What is certain is that, with the last charge of the French cavalry, the square collapsed in on itself and, in the initial stages of the retreat, battalion-sized knots of red-coated infantry fought their way eastwards, trying to gain Vezon and safety.

For the second time that day, the bottleneck between Fontenoy and the Bois de Barry became a major hindrance to the attacking troops, with Saxe now trying to push over 30 battalions of

The sole known surviving colour of a unit of the Irish Brigade, this battalion colour of the Dillon regiment would have been carried at the forefront of the regiment as it crashed into the British Guards. (Image copyright and reproduced with kind permission of the National Museum of Ireland, Dublin)

infantry through a gap that, just hours before, had been negotiated with difficulty by an Allied column but six battalions wide.

Artillery and baggage by now abandoned, the Allies began to regain their cohesion the farther east they reached, and as the French pursuit slackened off, units were able to reorganize themselves, but there was no way in which they could cleanly disengage from the enemy as the Grassins having swept the Austrian *Freikompagnien* aside, added their fire to the storm engulfing the retreating troops.

To buy time and cover the retreat, the Earl of Crawford rode up with his cavalry brigades and, knowing that there was no way to avoid the enemy cannon fire, simply threw his men into the enemy ranks hoping that their freshness would make the difference and stem the tide. Slicing into the French infantry, the British horsemen initially had the better of the combat, but as they pushed farther ahead, the space became more contracted and with little room to manoeuvre they began to take casualties – Crawford himself narrowly missed being knocked from his horse, whilst Königsegg, caught up in the fighting, escaped only by clinging precariously onto a trooper's saddle.

From his position above Fontenoy, Saxe could see that there was nothing more that could be done. He had fought the field engagement that he had sought and had gained the incontrovertible victory that had been denied him for so long, but his men were exhausted and with the Anglo-Hanoverian cavalry on the field, an overzealous pursuit could easily turn into a rout and snatch the laurels of victory from his hands. He had done enough to secure his objectives and, at shortly after 2.00pm, it was time enough to greet his adopted king and proclaim his victory.

Slowly the two armies separated and, as his troops passed through Vezon, Cumberland detailed four battalions, supported by the Austrian dragoons, to hold the town and act as a rearguard. Then, after a rushed conference at the roadside, he conveyed his intentions to Waldeck on a hastily scribbled note: 'Your Highness, I am going to place the Army under the protection of the guns of Ath. William'.

The note came as a clear relief to Waldeck, who believed – possibly rightly – that his troops, shaken by their earlier experiences, would baulk at being ordered into a third attack on the seemingly impregnable French positions. Accordingly, he now conducted a textbook disengagement, with the artillery moving back to Bourgeon, followed firstly by the infantry and finally by the cavalry, who remained in position to deter any enemy pursuit. Once contact had been successfully broken, Waldeck led his command back along its original line of advance, via Maubray and Wasmes, before swinging north to catch up with the remainder of the army.

On the ridgeline, and glancing down at the detritus of the Allied retreat, Saxe gave orders for a number of cavalry units to venture down to secure the abandoned artillery and munition wagons, and to make provision for the gathering of the dead and wounded of both sides. To cover this operation, he then ordered the Grassins forward to engage the Allied rearguard, which slipped away after a desultory firefight.

The retreat to Ath was naturally an emotional one. Cumberland's beloved redcoats had performed unbelievably, maintaining discipline even when their ranks were broken by the enemy, and fighting their way to safety. Whilst for the British – officers and rank and file alike – the Hanoverian contingent had now paid in blood for their 'conduct' at Dettingen. But for the men of the right wing, whether British or Hanoverian, the battle had been lost not where they themselves had fought but where, in their view, the Dutch had failed to fight. Indeed, the animosity was such that the army had to march in two bodies, not because of the state of the roads, but rather to avoid violence between the troops. Wedges were being driven between the contingents, which no diplomatic whitewashing of the official correspondence could resolve, divisions which would have consequences not just during the remainder of 1745, but also in the coming years when Saxe would complete his conquest of the Austrian Netherlands.

For Saxe, his ride to the royal headquarters was one of pure triumph, despite the polite smiles from many of those present, he knew that – with a number of notable exceptions – they were as much his enemies as the Allies had been and he had beaten them all. Approaching King Louis XV and the Dauphin, Saxe doffed his hat and bowed uncomfortably in his saddle, and sweeping has arm towards the east he rose again with the words, 'Your Majesty, I give you Victory!'

Belying his physical condition, this 19th-century watercolour shows an exhausted Saxe – possibly strapped into the saddle – riding up to the royal party in order to present Louis XV with the news of a hard fought, and at times unexpected, French victory.

The Spoils of War. This painting by Horace Vernet depicts the scale of the victory with a plethora of military loot. In the foreground, Saxe – on foot – presents King Louis XV with various battlefield trophies, whilst behind him the Maison du Roi leads the celebrations. In reality, and because of his infirmity, Saxe had been released from the obligation of dismounting in the presence of the king, and only one British colour was captured by the French. (Galerie de Batailles, Palace of Versailles)

'GOD SAVE IRELAND' – BOIS DE BARRY, APPROXIMATELY 1.15PM, TUESDAY 11 MAY 1745 (PP. 86–87)

Having reorganized his forces for what should have been a decisive attack upon the Allied column, Saxe had to go through the anguish of seeing his plan founder because of an unauthorized attack by the Comte d'Apcher whose men had compromised the passage of the Irish Brigade.

Their path finally clear and led by the Viscount Clare and Count Thomond, the Irish charged forward, crashing into the ranks of the enemy Guards (1) who had earlier swept aside the French front line – including the Gardes Françaises and the Gardes Suisses and threatening the Armée de Flandres with defeat.

As the Irishmen surged forward, tradition has it that a cry went up from their ranks *'Cuimhnígí ar Luimneach agus ar fheall na Sasanach!'* which translates as 'Remember Limerick and the Saxon perfidy', a potent reminder of what many believed to have been a deliberate breach of the treaty that ended the Williamite War in 1690.

Attacking in two 'divisions', the first comprising the regiments of Berwick, Lally and Rooth and the second those of Bulkeley, Dillon (2) and Clare, the Irishmen crashed into the British line, the fierce scrum being an almost immediate stalemate with neither side being able to gain the advantage.

The fighting was fierce, and here we see Colonel James Dillon (3) being killed instantly by a musket ball to the head, his men scarcely breaking ranks as they close with the foe (4). The Irish attack serves to pin the British Guardsmen in position, thereby achieving Saxe's aim of stopping the column dead in its tracks, and giving him the chance of committing other units to the combat at other points on the Allied perimeter, a series of hammer-blows designed to crack the Anglo-Hanoverian ranks and allow the French to convert a retreat into a rout.

THE AFTERMATH

Having successfully disengaged from battle, Cumberland was still of the belief that Saxe's primary aim was to destroy the Pragmatic Army as a fighting force, and he resolved to use any delays in a French pursuit to push his men hard, driving them towards the fortress of Ath, where he planned to rest and reorganize his forces whilst taking stock of the situation to develop a suitable strategy to prevent the enemy from capitalizing upon his victory. Although several reasons have been postulated about why Saxe failed to press home his advantage, ranging from his deteriorating health to a cautious respect for the British, who had not only almost performed the impossible but who still – if only from a distance – seemed prepared for further fighting. The simple truth is that the French were themselves far too exhausted and disorganized to mount an effective pursuit. In addition to this, it must be understood that Tournai was the prize, not a battlefield victory, and that Saxe had left the bare minimum of troops to maintain the siege whilst he defeated Cumberland and, that achieved, he now needed to bring the siege to a successful conclusion.

Saxe was more than content to allow the Allies to withdraw and, after drawing upon the garrison of Ath for further supplies, Cumberland withdrew north-east towards Lessines, ever hopeful that his opponent would continue to occupy himself with Tournai and give the Allies not only the time to make good their battlefield losses, but also to repair the rifts that were appearing in the Pragmatic Alliance.

Eleven days after the battle upon which his whole strategy had hinged, the city of Tournai itself surrendered to Saxe, with the Dutch garrison withdrawing into the citadel and the Marshal allowing its commander to send a messenger to The Hague requesting permission to surrender 'on terms'. The petition was ultimately denied and on 1 June formal siege operations recommenced. The garrison held out bravely for a further two and a half weeks, but with no chance of relief and with the outer defences in ruins, capitulation was inevitable and, on 19 June, the French took control of the citadel, to all intents and purposes fulfilling Saxe's plan of campaign. As the terms of capitulation meant that the Dutch garrison would not bear arms against France or her allies until 1 January 1747, they were eventually sent to England in order to release British troops for active service either on the Continent or ultimately against Prince Charles Edward Stuart.

The capture of Tournai meant that the French still had two or three months' grace before the end of the campaigning season, and Saxe meant to make the most of them by capturing Ath and widening the breach in the enemy defensive screen and for the second time he used a legitimate objective

The conquest of the Austrian Netherlands

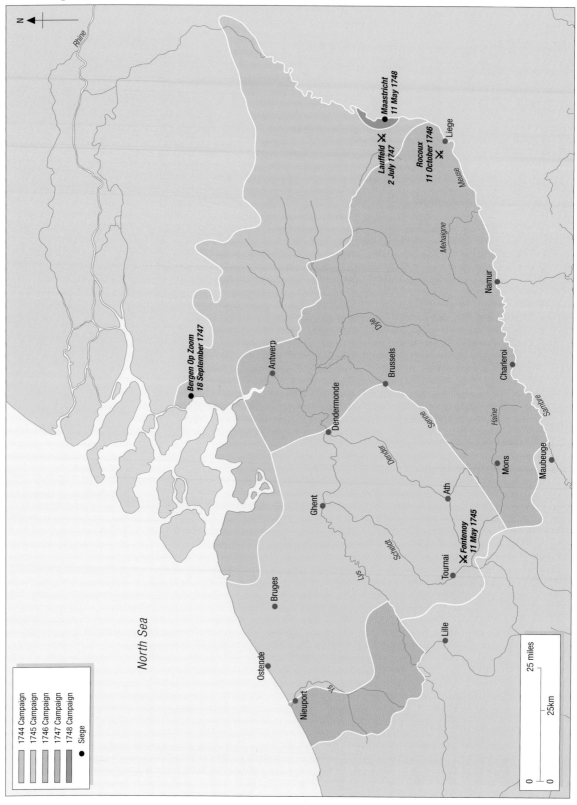

N ←

Rhine

● Maastricht
11 May 1748

✗ *Laurfeld*
2 July 1747

Liege

Rocoux
11 October 1746 ✗

Meuse

Mehaigne

Namur

Dyle

● *Bergen Op Zoom*
18 September 1747

Antwerp ●

Brussels ●

Charleroi

Dendermonde

Senne

Haine

Sambre

Dender

Ath

Mons

Maubeuge

Ghent

✗ *Fontenoy*
11 May 1745

Scheldt

Tournai

Lys

Bruges ●

Lille ●

North Sea

Ostende ●

Lys

Nieuport

1744 Campaign
1745 Campaign
1746 Campaign
1747 Campaign
1748 Campaign
● Siege

25 miles

25Km

0

0

90

as a piece of misdirection – whilst the main army marched east, several columns were detached to engage the Allied garrisons left in the French rear. Bypassing Oudenaarde, 5,000 men under Löwendahl force-marched deep into enemy territory, appearing without warning before the walls of Ghent and swarming over the defences before the garrison could react. Shortly afterwards Bruges fell without a shot being fired and over the following weeks Dendermonde, Nieuport, Ostende, Oudenaarde and Passchendaele all capitulated to the French.

Having invested Ath on 26 September and content to let the siege run its inevitable course, it was clear that Saxe had delivered upon all of the promises that he had made – the Allies had been decisively beaten in the field and, not only had Tournai been captured, but several other fortresses had also been taken and Western Flanders now lay firmly in French hands. It was the perfect springboard for future operations to capture Brussels and drive upon the port of Antwerp, severing Britain's most direct point of access to her allies. And with Britain's attention fixed upon the Low Countries, there was always the opportunity to increase the pressure even further by allowing 'Bonnie Prince Charlie' and his supporters to sail. If the Jacobites could draw sufficient British troops into a fruitless campaign in Scotland, it would stretch the enemy even further and increase the chances of success for further French operations.

In the opposing camp, the situation remained dire – the least of the problems being the replacement of men and materiel. The withdrawal to Ath had been acrimonious in the extreme and the subsequent 'blamestorming' had intensified. The British and Dutch, conveniently forgetting that the Austrians had counselled a Fabian strategy until reinforcements could be brought up to the front, castigated Vienna for having too few troops defending their own territory. The defence of Tournai had occasioned severe criticism from London for having been 'ineffective', whilst the government in The Hague baulked at the fact that it would have to pay the upkeep of several thousand troops who could take no active part in the war, preferring that they should have gone into captivity instead, where they would have become a charge upon the French treasury.

On 8 October 1745, Ath capitulated to the Marquis de Clérmont-Gallerande, effectively signalling the end of the campaign and, whilst the army went into winter quarters and many of his senior officers were given leave of absence, Saxe made his personal headquarters at Ghent. Once again rumours of his ill health and imminent demise soon began to surface, but amongst the news of sickness and abandonment of military duty, he was once more at work making plans and refining them. For 1746 he planned another coup – a quick campaign to capture Brussels before the enemy could react and mobilize their forces from their winter cantonments. It would be the second step in a journey which would end at Maastricht when, on 11 May 1748 – three years to the day after his victory at Fontenoy – he would complete the conquest of the Austrian Netherlands and give France a much-needed bargaining counter during the negotiations which would result in the 1748 Treaty of Aix-la-Chapelle (Aachen).

Contemporary map showing the defensive trace constructed by the Comte de la Vauguyon. Originally the village was occupied by the four battalions of the Brigade du Dauphin supported by eight cannon, but during the course of the battle more artillery was brought forward to bolster the defences. (Service Historique de la Défense, Château de Vincennes)

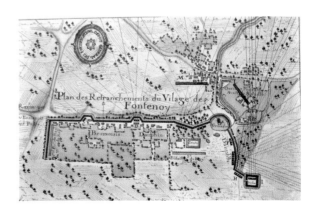

THE BATTLEFIELD TODAY

The Price. This painting by Philippoteaux shows King Louis XV and the Dauphin on the battlefield on the evening of the battle, the occasion being when the king gave his son the advice about the true nature of military glory. It should be noted that the escort party carries more captured British colours than were actually taken during the battle.

Unfortunately, the battlefield of Fontenoy has become a casualty of modern industrial development. It lies in a region designated as the closest area to Paris in which cement could be manufactured, and so several industrial plants ring the area. Of more modern creation, a sugar factory now obscures most of the site where the Anglo-Hanoverians struggled with the French counterattacks, and major road and rail links bisect other parts of the battlefield especially near the area where the Dutch made their ill-fated advance between Péronnes and Bourgeon.

That said, much of the battlefield remains accessible by car and both the author and artist are deeply grateful to Alain Bonnet and Alain Tripnaux who readily gave much of their time to guide us around the battlefield on consecutive days, answering our many questions about the battlefield and

allowing us to take the various location photographs which are included within this book. Many local landmarks can be made out from the contemporary paintings of the battlefield and, using these as a key or waypoint, the visitor can easily – despite the modern developments – envisage the progress of both armies at crucial points during the battle. Indeed, although the ground level has changed since the summer of 1745, the view across the open fields where the Dutch attacks were torn apart by artillery fire or the constricted area in which the Anglo-Hanoverian column forced its way and the French launched attack after attack cannot fail to stir the imagination.

The Nationaal Geografisch Instituut or Institut Géographique National in Brussels produces maps of the region in the various standard scales, and, at time of writing, a number of historical maps could be viewed online on its website (www.ngi.be).

FURTHER READING

A List of the Colonels, Lt-Colonels, Majors, Captains, Lieutenants and Ensigns of His Majesty's forces on the British Establishment 1740, London (1740)

Barrière, M.F., *Mémoires du Maréchal Duc de Richelieu*, (3 vols) Paris (1869)

Blackmore, David, *Destructive & Formidable: British Infantry Firepower 1642–1765*, Pen & Sword Books, Barnsley (2014)

Bland, Maj-Gen Humphrey, *A Treatise of Military Discipline* (6th Edition) London (1746)

Bois, Jean-Pierre, *Fontenoy 1745 – Louis XV, arbiter d'Europe*, Paris (2012)

Bonnet, Alain & Ó hAnnracháin, Eoghan (eds), *Fontenoy 11 Mai 1745*, Tournai (2015)

Broglie, Albert, Duc de, *Maurice de Saxe et le Marquis d'Argenson* (2 vols) Paris (1891)

Browning, Reed, *The War of The Austrian Succession*, St. Martin's Press, New York (1995)

Campbell, Archibald, *William Augustus, Duke of Cumberland – General Orders 1745–47*, London (1876)

Charteris, Evan, *William Augustus, Duke of Cumberland – His Early Life & Times (1726–48)*, London (1913)

Chartrand, René, *Louis XV's Army (1): Cavalry & Dragoons*, Osprey Publishing, Oxford (1996)

Chartrand, René, *Louis XV's Army (2): French Infantry*, Osprey Publishing, Oxford (1996)

Chartrand, René, *Louis XV's Army (3): Foreign Infantry*, Osprey Publishing, Oxford (1997)

Chartrand, René, *Louis XV's Army (4): Light Troops & Specialists*, Osprey Publishing, Oxford (1997)

Coxe, William, *The Administration of the Rt. Hon Henry Pelham* (2 vols) London (1829)

De la Fuye, Maurice, *Fontenoy 1745*, Paris (1945)

Deligne, Charles & Tripnaux, Alain, *1745 Tournai et Fontenoy – un siège, une bataille*, Tournai (2015)

Duffy, Christopher, *The Military Experience in the Age of* Reason, Routledge & Kegan Paul, London (1987)

Forbes, Archibald, *The Black Watch – The record of an historic regiment*, New York (1896)

Fortescue, Sir John W., *A History of the British Army* (Vol. 2, Part 1) London (1899)

Gandilhon, Denis, *Fontenoy – France dominating Europe* (Trans. Alan McKay) Histoire et Collections, Paris (2008)

Hamilton, Sir F.W., *The Origins & History of the First or Grenadier Guards* (3 Vols) London (1874)

Hödl, Rudolf, (k.u.k. Kriegsarchiv) *Österreichischer Erbfolgekrieg 1740–48* (Vol 9) Vienna (1914)

London Gazette, 7–11 May 1745

London Gazette, 18–22 June 1745

MacKinnon, Col. Daniel, *Origins & Services of the Coldstream Guards* (2 vols) London (1833)

Mercure de France, May 1745

Mercure de France, June 1745 (2 vols)

Mercure de France, July 1745

Mercure de France, August 1745

Mouillard, Lucien, *The French Army of Louis XV* (Trans. George F. Nafziger) Nafziger Collection, West Chester (2004)

Nosworthy, Brent, *The Anatomy of Victory: Battle Tactics 1689–1763*, Hippocrene Books, New York (1992)

O'Callaghan, John Cornelius, *History of the Irish Brigades in the Service of France*, Irish University Press, Shannon (1969)

Ordonnance du Roy, *Portant création d'un régiment de Troupes Légères tant á pied qu'á cheval, sous le nom d'Arquebusiers de Grassin*, Paris (1744)

Ordonnance du Roy, *Portant nouveau réglement sur le port et l'usage des cuirasses*, Paris (1744)

Pajol, C.P.V, Comte de, *Les Guerres sous Louis XV* (7 vols) Paris (1881–91)

Reid, Stuart, *King George's Army 1740–93 (1) Infantry*, Osprey Publishing, Oxford (1995)

Reid, Stuart, *King George's Army 1740–93 (2)*, Osprey Publishing, Oxford (1995)

Reid, Stuart, *King George's Army 1740–93 (3)*, Osprey Publishing, Oxford (1996)

Relation de la Bataille de Fontenoy, Lyon (1745)

Relation de la Campagne en Brabant et en Flandres de 1745, 1746, 1747, Paris (1746–48)

Rogers, Col. H.C.B., *The British Army of the Eighteenth Century*, London (1977)

Rolt, Richard, *Memoirs of the Life of John Lindesay, Earl of Craufurd and Lindesay*, London (1753)

Rousseau, *Abbé de, Campagnes du Roy en 1744 & 1745* (3rd edition) Paris (1746)

Saxe, Maurice, *Comte de, Lettres et Memoires choisis des papiers originaux du Maréchal de Saxe* (4 vols) Paris (1794)

Saxe, Maurice, *Comte de, Reveries on the Art of War* (Trans. Brigadier-General Thomas R. Philips), Dover Publications, New York (2007)

Sheehan, Vincent, *A Day of Battle*, Literary Guild of America, New York (1938)

Sinety, André Louis Woldemar Alphée, Marquis de, *La Vie du Maréchal de Lowendal* (Vols 1 & 2) Paris (1867–68)

Skrine, Francis Henry, *Fontenoy*, William Blackwood & Sons, Edinburgh (1906)

Starkey, Armstrong, *War in the Age of Enlightenment, 1700–1789*, Westport (2003)

Townsend, Lt.-Col. C.V.F., *The Military Life of Field Marshal George, 1st Marquess Townsend*, London (1901)

Waldeck, Karl August, Fürst von, *Memoires sur les Campagnes en Flandres de 1745–46–47*, Göttingen (1803)

Weaver, Lawrence, *The Story of the Royal Scots (The Lothian Regiment)*, London (1913)

White, Jon Manchip, *Marshal of France – The Life and Times of Maurice, Comte de Saxe (1696–1750)*, Rand, McNally & Co, New York (1962)

Whitworth, Rex, *Field Marshal Lord Ligonier*, Oxford University Press, London (1958)

Whitworth, Rex, *William Augustus, Duke of Cumberland*, Pen & Sword Books, Barnsley (1992)

Zwitzer, H.L. with Hoffenaar, Jan and van der Spek, C.W. (eds), *Het Staatse Leger* (Vol. 9) Amsterdam (2016)

INDEX